Thames Crossings

A photographic journey over and under the River Thames from source to estuary

by Mark Chesterton

Copyright

Thames Crossings

www.claykettlebooks.com

e-mail: claykettlebooks@gmail.com

Design, Layout & Text: Copyright 2016 © Clay Kettle Books

Photographs: Copyright 2016 © Mark Chesterton

Maps & Graphics: Copyright 2016 © Kate Chesterton

All rights reserved. No part of this publication may be reproduced, stored in a retrieval system or transmitted by any means electronic, mechanical, photocopying, recording or otherwise without the prior permission of the copyright holder.

Clay Kettle Books hereby exclude all liability to the extent permitted by law for any errors or omissions in this book and for any loss, damage or expense (whether direct or indirect) suffered by a third party relying on information contained in this book.

ISBN-13: 978-1533371263

The Author

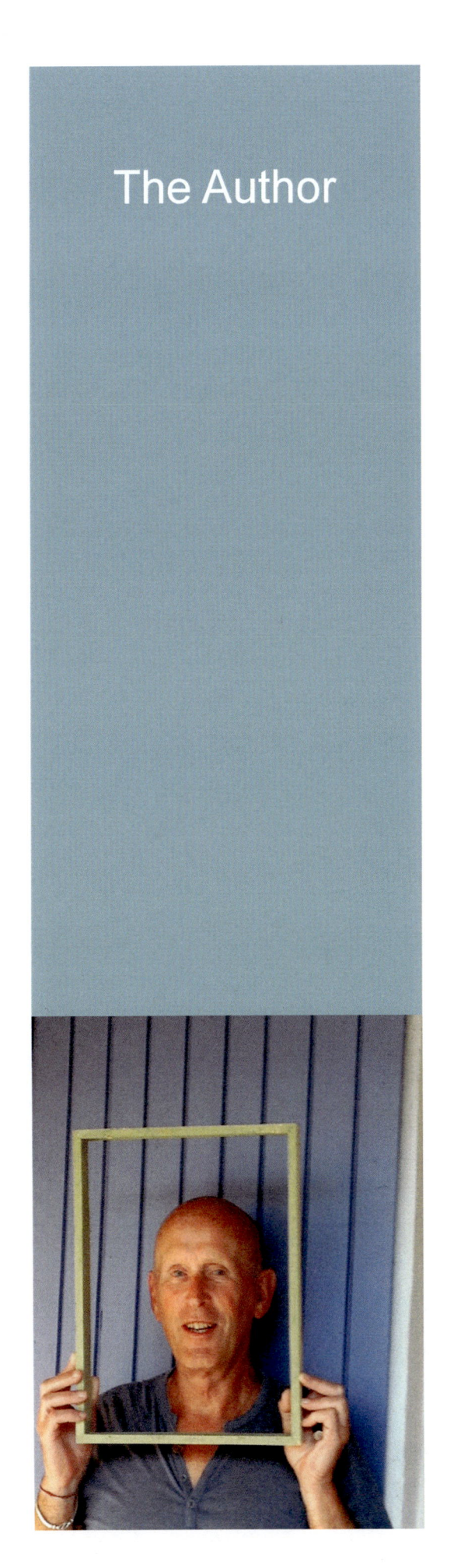

About Mark Chesterton

Mark is a 'local boy' with many close connections to the Thames Valley. He grew up in Reading. Bit by bit he moved along the river, living just outside Goring-on-Thames and then Benson and Ewelme before finally settling in Oxford in 2001. He started teaching in Reading and then moved into Oxfordshire where he has taught ever since, for the last 25 years as head teacher of a large primary school in Oxford itself. Retirement has given him opportunities to develop his passion for travel, photography, history and writing.

Contents

- 5 Introduction
- 6 Locks & Weirs
- 7 The Tow Path
- 8 Fords & Ferries
- 9 The Crossings
- 10 The Upper Thames
- 34 The Middle Reaches
- 72 The Tidal Thames
- 100 Controlling the River
- 101 Historical Sources
- 102 Index

Thanks

I must thank a number of people - Trish and Wendy who did sterling work to decipher the scrawl in my notebook and translate it into legible script; my daughter, Kate, who designed the maps and graphics; Ros, who introduced me to the world of production and publishing; and Hazel who provided invaluable advice on layout and production issues as well as oodles of support. Thanks to you all.

Introduction

There are so many facets to the River Thames as it courses and wiggles and winds its way down from its source above Kemble, to its estuary into the North Sea. Each one captures its own special glimpse of colour and texture and smell and shape and motion.

There is the calm isolation along its upper reaches where the only humanity is the occasional passing boat and a wave from its wheel house or the face of a lockkeeper, appearing from his hut or garden to operate the gate mechanism. The peaceful passage of gently swirling currents glug past colourful communities of tied boats and barges and back gardens of flat lawns which reveal panoramic windows into rooms of chintzy settees and garden furniture. Stretching meadows of buttercups and wild flowers host cotton wool clumps of hedgerows and woodland which, in places, change to clagging, muddy farmland, holding onto towering fields of grasping maize or hosting surly cattle chewing the cud.

The gravel towpath pushes through the towns and cities of this land, keeping the widening river company where ever it can. As it pushes its waters along, the river hosts gleaming hire boats, painted canal barges, private pleasure cruisers, sleek rowing eights, rusting work horses, reassuring river police vessels, anchored fishing skiffs, fun-ridden row boats.

Along the built up banks range the tenements and the backs of posh private dwellings and businesses ranging from classy pubs to posh riverside restaurants to sprawling shopping centres to scruffy terminals and depots. The past remains of livelihoods and trades and occupations are still in evidence around docks and locks and wharves and quays. Apartment and office blocks tower and grow like Jack's beans, unencumbered, into the heavens to gain full advantage from their riverside settings.

Over the centuries the Thames has both united and separated. Merchants, traders, monarchs, priests, manufacturers, farmers have all taken full advantage of its journey through the heart of England. It becomes a barrier only when you wish to cross and it is then that local ingenuity and wealth work together to devise a suitable method to get over this watery ribbon of an obstacle.

This is a photographic record of all the crossings that are still in public use today, accompanied by some historical information for each one. After all, they have witnessed many of the key events that have shaped our land. I have visited every one. I hope you find this journey as interesting as I have done and that my pictures and words inspire you to get out and explore the river and its banks.

Locks & Weirs

The River Thames is the longest river in England and the second longest in the United Kingdom. It flows 215 miles (346 km) from its source in Gloucestershire to its estuary on the east coast.

It is navigable up to Cricklade for small boats and to Letchlade for larger vessels. The fall on the non-tidal part of the river from the source to Teddington is 104 metres. There are in all 47 locks on the river, each with adjacent weirs to control the flow of water, some of which can be used by the public to cross the river on foot. The main purpose of the weirs is to control the flow of water down the river course, particularly when there is a risk of flooding. Beyond Teddington the river is tidal with a difference between low and high tide as great as 7 metres at London Bridge. Richmond Lock, the only lock in the tidal section, was built to maintain a navigable depth of water upstream and to ensure that there is always, whatever the tide, at least a 1.72m depth in the river between Richmond and Teddington.

From ancient times there have been many obstructions across the river, from fish pounds and millers' weirs, to outcrops of rock and causeways of harder soil. In 1215 Magna Carta stated that the Thames' weirs would be abolished. This never happened.

In the Middle Ages, the fall in the middle and upper sections of the river was used to drive watermills and involved constructing weirs to divert water into the mills to power machinery. These caused obstructions and so locks were built alongside them to enable boats to move between levels.

The first locks were flash locks. These were made up of 'fences' of wooden railings called paddles stretching across the river. Sections were removed to allow boats through. A boat moving downstream would wait above the lock while some paddles were lifted out. This would allow a 'flash' of water to rush through taking the boat with it. Vessels moving upstream would have to be winched or towed through the gap. These were difficult to operate. They were also unpopular with the mill owners as the reduced flow to their mills resulted in the loss of power. Frequently there was a walkway over the top and although rather precarious, this could be used to cross between the banks. Fish traps, osieries and 'bucks' for catching eels were frequently located near weirs.

The difficulty of using flash locks, and the consequent loss of water, eventually led to their replacement with pound locks, whose basic design has not changed since they were first used in medieval China during the Song Dynasty (960–1279 AD). Lock gates are still based on Leonardo da Vinci's design from the 1500s.

In 1871 Taunt writes that the flash lock at Eaton (Hart's) Weir was notoriously difficult to negotiate due to a fall of 3 feet:

'I recollect one winter in passing this very weir, when lying on my back in the boat to get through, scraping a fair amount of skin off my nose and face through contact with the bridge whilst going under it.'

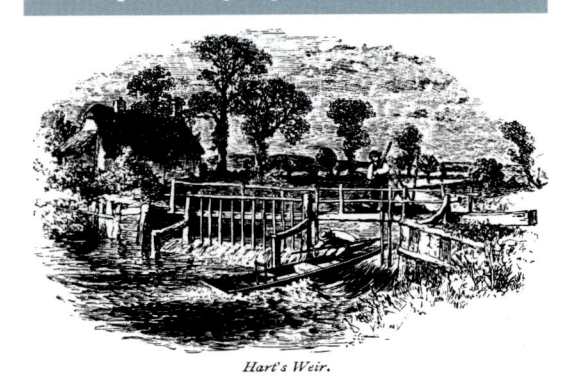

Hart's Weir.

© Oxfordshire History Centre

The Tow Path

An Island on the Thames near Park Place, Oxfordshire by William Havell (1782-1857)

© Tyne & Wear Archives & Museums/Bridgeman Images

Paths, on the banks of the river, enabled beasts of burden to travel easily. Then boats and barges became the main method of transporting goods around the country. They were towed or pulled up the river with pulling power provided from the bank by human pullers, in the form of Towing Path Companies, teams of horses or even early steam vehicles.

Barges could, and did, use sails but frequently the winds were not favourable and the river was too narrow for tacking. So gangs of men bow-hauled the boats. River banks were privately owned and so these teams of men made their way up the river as best they could and were often forced to change banks if landowners refused to let them pass or if they levied tolls to cross their land. When horses took the place of Towing Path Companies they had to follow the same routes and larger ferries or bridges were used to cross them to the other side.

After the Industrial Revolution towing became obsolete when engines were fitted to boats. The railways then became the main, quicker, method of transportation for goods and passengers.

The Thames Path was first proposed in 1948 and eventually opened in 1996. It follows the length of the river from the source to the Thames Barrier. In most places it follows the towpath but where this is not possible, due to obstructive landowners or where ferries no longer exist, diversions are made away from the river, as at Whitchurch and at Shiplake. In other places new footbridges were built to take the Thames Path across to the other bank, as at Temple Bridge in Hurley in 1989.

Fords & Ferries

Old Moulsford Ferry 1887—1897

© Oxfordshire History Centre

In early days the simplest method to ferry someone from bank to bank was by piggy back (*pick-a-back*). In other words, a strong ferryman would simply pick up a passenger and carry them across the river. Some even used stilts to keep themselves above water level. Early fords, weirs and bridges took the form of stepping stones, the build-up of river debris behind fallen trees, loosely woven hurdles which would trap river debris until it was strong enough to walk on or willow baskets filled with stones.

The primary purpose of a ferry is to enable passengers, animals, wagons, coaches, carts and other vehicles to cross the river safely. Flat-bottomed, square-ended, timber punts were the typical ferry used on the Thames. These were mainly 24 feet long and 3 feet wide, with cross-bands linking sides of hardwood, normally ash. They were cheaper to build than row boats. The technique used to propel them was called 'shoving'. This required the ferrymen to walk up and down each side of the punt, at the same time pushing against the pole to propel the craft. One man could shove a coach and horse or 20 passengers. 50 passengers required two men to provide the shoving power. It was only after 1860 that punting became a recreational activity rather than a way to cross the river.

There were other types of ferry depending on their purpose and cargo. These ranged from a simple row boat propelled by two oars, to a flat-bottomed punting barge described above, to an overhead rope strung across the river with the ferryman hauling hand over hand, to a chain strung along the bottom of the river and pulled up with a spiked wheel attached to the boat. Larger boats might be attached by chain or rope to a windlass located on each bank and cranked over by hand.

The Crossings

There are over 200 crossings over or under the river. 152 are described in this book. I do not include the many simple plank bridges used by landowners in the highest reaches of the river nor service tunnels used by service personnel nor those tunnels that form part of London's underground railway system.

Throughout history crossings were built across the river and acted, amongst other things, as a source of income from traffic crossing on it or passing under it. Some landowners refused to allow a towpath over their land and so, at the boundary to their estates, towing animals had to be crossed over to the other side of the river and continue their journey on the other bank. Farmers, villagers, townsfolk would cross to access pastures, fields, local services or families on the other side, to attend church or, maybe, to have a pint or two of ale at their local hostelry. Traders and merchants would transport goods across to reach markets and fairs. As towns expanded across the river new crossings were required to enable people to get to work in the increasing number of factories and businesses.

Many foot crossings were established across the locks and weirs that were built on the non-tidal river.

Many of the present road bridges over the river are on the sites of earlier fords, ferries and wooden structures. Timber piles dating from the Bronze Age have been found just upstream from Vauxhall Bridge. They can be seen at low tide and are believed to form part of the structure of the first bridge across the Thames. The Romans constructed timber bridges at the site of London Bridge, the narrowest part of the river, and at Staines Bridge. At Folly Bridge in Oxford the remains of a Saxon framework can be seen, and medieval structures such as New Bridge are still in use today. During the 18th century, many stone and brick road bridges were built to replace existing timber structures.

The development of the railways resulted in a spate of bridge building in the 19th century using the new materials of the Industrial Revolution - iron and steel.

Four historic ferries still operate on the river in and around London carrying passengers or vehicles across the widening flow.

In 2016 plans were published to create new crossings in the east part of London: Silvertown Tunnel to connect the Greenwich with the Royal Docks via a four-lane road under the Thames, a cycling and walking bridge linking Rotherhithe and Canary Wharf, an extension of the Docklands Light Railway, a London Overground crossing and a new ferry from North Greenwich to the Isle of Dogs.

Waterloo Bridge 1815

Westminster City Archives

The Upper Thames

Kemble to Oxford

This section covers the river's upper course, from the source near Kemble, down past Oxford. The river, in its very upper reaches, can be more of a muddy trickle than what might be recognised as a river or even a stream and can be completely dry during the summer months. By Ashton Keynes it has become a shallow stream even during the driest of summers. The Thames continues its journey eastwards through fields and meadows and past farms and estates and hamlets and villages and the small town of Cricklade. The river becomes navigable for larger vessels from Letchlade. It flows under ancient bridges, over the site of fords and ferries, through locks and cuts and chases and over weirs and steps and runs, until the college and church spires of Oxford appear above the meadows.

Crossing	Date
A433 (Fosse Way) Bridge, Kemble	
A429 Road Bridge, Kemble	
Ewan Bridges	
Neigh Bridges	
Bridges in Ashton Keynes	
Hailstone House Footbridge	
Midland & SW Junction Bridge	1884ff
North Meadow Footbridges, Cricklade	
Cricklade Town Bridge	1852
A419 Road Bridge, Cricklade	1988
Eysey Footbridge	
Water Eaton House Footbridge	
Castle Eaton Bridge	1893
Hannington Bridge	1841
Inglesham Roundhouse Footbridge	1789
Halfpenny Bridge, Letchlade	1792
St John's Bridge	1886
Bloomers Hole Footbridge	2000
Buscot Lock & Weir	1790
Eaton Hastings Footbridge	1936
Radcot Bridge	1200ish
Old Man's Footbridge	1894
Rushey Lock & Weir	1790
Tadpole Bridge	1796
Tenfoot Footbridge	1869
Shifford Cut Footbridge & Duxford Ford	1898
New Bridge	1250ish
Hart's Weir Footbridge	1879
Bablock Hythe Ferry Crossing Site	1279
Pinkhill Lock & Weir	1791
Swinford Toll Bridge	1769
Eynsham Lock & Weir	1928
Thames Bridge	1961
Godstow Bridge Part 1	<1645
Godstow Bridge Part 2	1792
Toll Bridge, Wolvercote (Airmen's Bridge)	1876
Medley Footbridge	1865
Osney Bridge, Oxford	1889
Osney Rail Bridge	1850
Gasworks Bridge	1886
Grandpont Bridge	1930s
Folly Bridge	1827
Donnington Bridge	1962

A433 (Fosse Way) Bridge, Kemble

Thames Head is a dry spring which some say is the source of our magnificent river. In open fields north west of Kemble a stone, shadowed by a small clump of trees, is inscribed with the words *'This stone was placed here to mark the source of the River Thames'*. Gentle undulations lead to a tangle of bushes lining the A433, originally a Roman Road called the Fosse Way, and then disappear into a brick-lined culvert.

However on the other side of the road, two fields further down is Lydwell Spring, an active spring from which the river flows and rather tentatively begins its journey, stopping off first in the confusion of lakes that make up the Cotswold Water Park.

Others argue that Seven Springs, north of Cirencester, is the true source. The River Churn flows south from here and also eventually enters the water park and joins the other stream just downstream from Cricklade.

A429 Road Bridge, Kemble

The first 'proper' bridge takes the A329 across the surprisingly wide, but shallow, river bed to the north of Kemble. It is a low, sturdy twin arched bridge, built out of stone, which, with some delusions of grandeur, rather grandly crosses the water course. The two arches stretch across the flat dip that passes as a river bed strewn with rocks and stones and vegetation, lacking an abundance of the one thing that would confirm it as the route of the Thames - water.

Ewan Bridges

Parker's Bridge, just outside of, and another unnamed bridge to the south of, the village of Ewan both carry a country road across the river bed.

Thames Crossings 11

The Bridges of Somerford Keynes

Depending on the season and the depth of the water table, the river course can be dry as it passes through the village of Somerford Keynes. Several small, timber footbridges arch over the channel where the young Thames has, during wetter times, churned out a flat river bed. Hollyhocks and foxgloves line this channel, a picture frame to their jigsaw-pretty cottages. Pedestrians are able to cross back and forth across the stoney river bed to reach the lakes and pathways of the Cotswold Water Park.

Neigh Bridges

These two bridges are on the edge of Cotswold Water Park just outside the village of Somerford Keynes. The two Neigh bridges, about 100 metres apart, cross this trickle that is called the Thames.

Surprisingly there seems to be a flow of water under the far bridge that takes the main road, rather than the stagnant pools that lead up to the Martian eyes of the first.

Bridges in Ashton Keynes

In and around the village of Ashton Keynes a number of flat, simple bridges carry small roads & paths over the shallow stream. Some of these enable villagers to pootle around the village, others allow householders to access their properties. In places the waters take their leave and disappear into inaccessible back gardens. The most picturesque stretch is in the village itself along Mill Lane. As the name suggests, a mill was built over the stream and the waters used to generate power.

B4696 Road Bridge   **Mill Walk Bridge**   **Mill Lane Bridge**   **Kent End Bridge**

Waterhay Bridge

Waterhay Bridge crosses the Thames near where Swill Brook joins the main river. Waterhay village now consists of a couple of farms and cottages on the south bank, although in the 13th Century, it was big enough to have a small church, little of which remains as it was dismantled and rebuilt up the road in Leigh. Amongst the fields each farm has a simple flat, normally concrete, bridge to enable cattle to access the northern meadows.

Hailstone House Footbridge

The footbridge at Hailstone House is of timber construction and takes an ancient track across the rushes-lined stream on the site of a Roman ford.

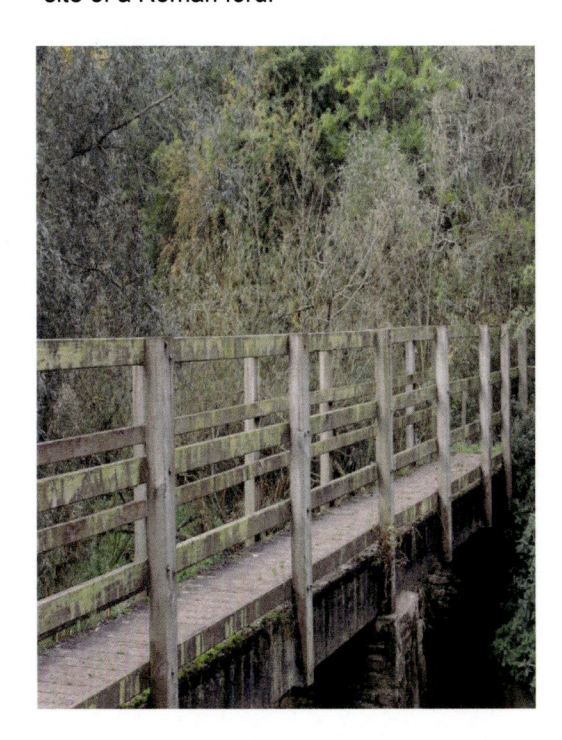

Midland & SW Junction Railway Bridge

Outside Cricklade a canal once crossed the river here within an aqueduct. When the canal closed, a bigger bridge was built to carry the Midland and South Western Junction Railway between Cheltenham and Andover. This, in its turn, closed in 1970. The crossing was then converted for use as a footpath and a cycleway route.

North Meadow Footbridge, Cricklade

This is another farm bridge but built of timber and with gates at each end. These prevent unauthorised access to the far meadows by cattle but enable walkers to return to the town on a very tranquil, circular walk.

North Meadow Farm Bridge

This is a simple concrete farm bridge which connects the town to the farm and meadows on the far side.

Cricklade Town Bridge

The present bridge was built in 1852 when local roads were diverted through the town. The original crossing at Cricklade was near the new A319 road bridge. Up until 1830 there was a thriving wharf here which had existed from Roman times. Small barges were able to reach the town carrying up to ten tons of goods. In 1984 a small, converted rowing boat carried a 'Token Ton' of goods up the river to Cricklade to maintain this tradition.

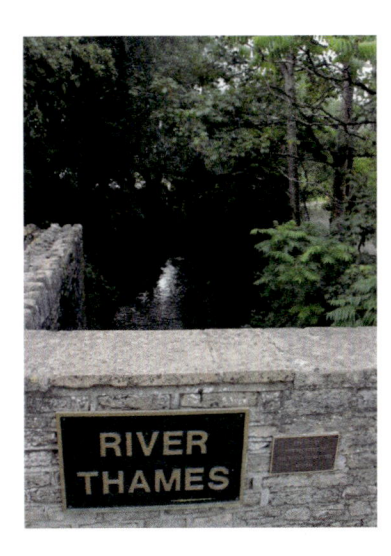

A419 Road Bridge

This is a modern, concrete road bridge opened in 1988. The A419 follows the Roman Ermin Street and the bridge probably coincides with an ancient crossing over the Thames. In 1692 Baskervile wrote : *'It is a footbridge built of wood for people to go over in time of floods, which has 22 passes for water between ye posts'*

Eysey Footbridge

This is an old plank bridge, now a more sturdy timber construction, which crosses the shallow, infant Thames to access the other bank. It is on the site of an ancient ford used by farmers and hunters alike.

Water Eaton House Bridge

This is a wooden bridge which enables cattle to cross the river and reach the meadows on the far side. It is downstream from what was Water Eaton House on the site of Water Eaton, or Nun Eaton, Mill which is mentioned in the Domesday Book. Godstow Priory, connected to the Abbey near Oxford, had a settlement here, with a mill and maybe a "house of mercy". A modern farmhouse now stands on the site.

Castle Eaton Bridge

This is an iron girder bridge built on brick piers in 1893 and strengthened in 2001. The river was originally crossed at the ancient ford in nearby Kempsford where the meadow by the church was used for the training of archers. The first mention of the bridge here was in 1692 when Baskervile wrote: *'Built wt timber stone peers and planks & railes tis about 73 yards over 34 arches for water to pass & at ye end of a long stone Casway a bridge of 2 arches. Postes between them make 8 Arches'*. In 1888 Paul Blake in his book The Thames: Oxford to its Source wrote: *'Castle Eaton Bridge was next passed after a long struggle with some cantankerous rush-beds with weeds intermingled'*.

A Thames Survey in 1929 stated: *'The old bridge was of timber with stone piers and stone causeway. It was replaced in 1893 by the present iron girder bridge with brick piers. The whole structure is of most deplorable design and painted a vermilion colour'*. In similar fashion it was described by Fred Thacker in 1920 as *'the present deplorable iron trough'*.

Hannington Bridge

The river is just about navigable from Lechlade up to Cricklade but only by rowing boats and not barges. Here the stream is fast and shallow making it difficult for river traffic. The stone bridge was built in 1841 and replaces earlier timber bridges. In 1941 it was rebuilt. The bridge has three small skew arches and a causeway on either side with flood arches.

In 1692 Baskerville wrote: *'Hannington Bridge is about 120 yards over the river & is built of partly stone peers partly timber posts between 4 great stone Peeres and 4 timbers. 8 Arches besides to vent water in time of floods. 16 in all. Horse and foot people go over bridge, carts, wagons, coaches go through water by ye bridge'*.

Inglesham Roundhouse Footbridge

This is cattle/pedestrian bridge of timber construction just downstream from where the Thames and Seven Canal joined the Thames. It replaces earlier bridges on either side of the canal entrance. The Roundhouse is one of five such buildings on the canal and served as a lengthsman's cottage. The ground floor was used for stabling animals, with living accommodation on the two floors above. The house was constructed within two years of the canal opening in 1789.

Halfpenny Bridge, Lechlade

Halfpenny Bridge is a bow backed, stone bridge built in 1792 to a design by James Hollingworth. Initially a toll was charged for pedestrians to cross. This was abolished in 1839 although it continued for animals until the 1870's. A small, square toll house is situated on the town side.

Lechlade is the start of the navigable Thames or, put another way, it is the highest point upstream that barges and larger vessels can reach easily. This, combined with the completion in 1789 of the Thames & Seven Canal which joined the river just above the town, meant that it became a busy inland port.

The bridge replaced the ferry that existed at the time, which was inadequate for the increase in trade that the canal bought. Park End Wharf, now Arkell's Riverside, used to be really busy with barge traffic.

A Lechlade bargee stated in 1793 that the chief goods he took to London were: *'Iron, Copper, Tin, manufactured and pig iron, Brass Spelter, Cannon, Cheese, Nails, all Iron goods and Bomb shells'*. He brought back *'Groceries, Deals, Foreign Timber, Merchandise of every kind, a few coals, and of late Raw Hides for Tewkesbury and Worcester and Gunpowder to Bristol and Liverpool'*.

St John's Bridge, near Lechlade

The Trout Inn - originally St John's Priory
1228 to 1472 - a hospital
1763 - a workhouse
1977 - a caravan park

The present bridge dates from 1879. The original bridge was built in 1229 by St John's Priory, on the line of an old ford that once stood nearby, close to where the Trout Inn now is. In 1245 Peter Fitzherbert was granted permission by Henry III to build a gate at the foot of the bridge in order to charge tolls for crossing.

Numerous kings, up to Henry VIII, granted the priory rights to toll travellers to help pay for repairs. From 1579 to 1629 entries on the Court Rolls of Shrivenham Manor identified individuals as being fined for not repairing the bridge.

In 1790 a cut was dug and a lock, the first pound lock on the river, and a weir were constructed. A Thames survey in 1929 states '*In 1795 the new bridge was built over the pound tail cut. The main bridge was rebuilt in 1820 and the lock cut bridge rebuilt in 1879: these last two comprise the existing satisfactory structure, all in stone, with one segmental arch over the main stream and weir and one similar arch over the lock cut*'.

The first lock house was built in 1830 when the lock keeper had to move out of the Trout Inn. The commissions rules at the time, prevented publicans from becoming lock keepers.

Baskervile wrote in 1690: [the bridge is] '*about 140 yards in length thwarting the River between Glocestershire and Berks, it has 11 arches to vent water in time of floods but 2 of these arches are great, built over the Mainstream where loaden boats go through. St John Bridge Fair is kept on the 29 August in the Meadow below ye bridge on the Glocester shire side, to which Oxford boats & others resort to sell Ale, Beef & Carrots, & to carry goods from this fair downstream. It is a great fair for Cattle and Cheese, and here you meet with brave sage cheese. No place elsewhere in England shews the like, much diversified in figures, green and white, as to round chees, and some in shape of Dolphins and Mermaids, as Country Carvers display them in Cheesefats.*'

We grant to you, that from the day of making these presents to the end of two years next following to be fully completed, you take by the hands of those in whom you confide, and for whom you will answer, for things carried over that Bridge to be sold, the following tolls: that is to say –

For ever horse-load of grass for sale, one farthing;
For every cart-load of grass for sale, one halfpenny;
For every horse, mare, ox, and cow for sale, one farthing;
For every hide of a horse and mare for sale, one farthing;
For every hundred-weight of skins of goats, stags, hinds, bucks and does, for sale, one halfpenny;
For every hundred-weight of skins of lambs, hares, rabbits, foxes, cats, and squirrels for sale, one farthing;
For every horse-load of cloth for sale, one halfpenny;
For every entire cloth for sale, one farthing;
For every hundred-weight of linen cloth, canvass, cloth of Ireland, Galway, and Worsted, one halfpenny;
For every cask of wine or ale for sale, one penny;
For every cart-load of honey for sale, one halfpenny;
For every trussel of cloths for sale, brought in a card, two pence;
Or every cart-load of lead for sale, one penny;
For avoirdupois, that is to say, for the hundred-weight, one penny;
For every poise of candles and tallow for sale, one farthing;
For every quarter of wood for sale, one halfpenny;
For every hundred-weight of alum, copperas, argol, and verdigris for sale, one farthing;
For 2000 onions for sale, one farthing;
For 10 sheaves of garlick for sale, one farthing;
For every 1000 of herrings for sale, one farthing;
For every cart-load of sea fish for sale, one penny;
For every horse-load of sea fish, one farthing;
For every 100 of boards for sale, one halfpenny;
For every mill-stone for sale, one farthing;
For every 1000 of faggots for sale, one penny;
For every quarter of salt for sale, one farthing;
For every poise of cheese or butter for sale, one farthing;
For every cart-load of fire-wood and coals for sale, one halfpenny;
For every quarter of bark for sale, one farthing;
For every 100weight of tin, brass or copper for sale, one halfpenny;
For every trussel of merchandise whatsoever for sale, one farthing;
For every other thing for sale of the value of 5 shillings not here specified and carried over that Bridge (except wool, fleeces, hides of oxon and cows, and iron,) one farthing.

Bloomers Hole Footbridge

The bridge, built of steel in 2000 and encased in wood to look like timber, carries the Thames Path across the river. The 2 x 27m x 8 tonne steel beams were put in place by a Chinook helicopter from RAF Brize Norton. Bloomers Hole is a wide bend just downstream from St John's Lock where the river meanders sharply. A cut to avoid the worst of these was muted in 1802 but it came to nothing and was not built.

Buscot Lock & Weir

This is the smallest lock on the Thames and was built in stone in 1790 by E. Loveden of Buscot Park. A cresting weir was created in 1979 when a cut was made through fields on the south side of the lock to create a weir pool and a picnic area, both now owned by the National Trust, as is the village of Buscot, with its tea rooms and small hotel. This is a lovely, peaceful spot with an abundance of wildlife - otters, red kites and kingfishers.

In 1780 the mansion and park at Buscot was built just above the lock. In 1813 a Cheese Wharf was established here, rented by cheese mongers in London to receive cheeses from the locality. Thousands of tons of cheese were sent down the Thames each year.

In 1859 Robert Tertius Campbell bought the villages of Buscot and Easton Hastings. He set about turning the rundown estate into a marvel of modern Victorian industry. He drained the land and dug a 20 acre reservoir installing three large water wheel diver pumps (12 feet high, 16 feet wide) to fill it. He grew sugar beet on the irrigated land, collected the crop with a light railway and 3 locomotives, took it to the distillery on the right bank just above Buscot Lock where he produced alcohol which he sold to France for 2/6d. He also manufactured and sold oil cake, gas, fertiliser and vitriol. By 1879 the estate was no longer making a profit and the whole scheme was scrapped. Buscot House remains open to the public.

Eaton Hastings Footbridge

This is a wooden footbridge built in 1936 on the site of a flash lock in a weir known, in 1749, as Hart's Weir. In the past, buildings here included a weir-keeper's cottage and a walkway across the top of the weir to the Anchor Inn on the other bank which has since burned down. A cut was dug at this point to power two waterwheels for the Buscot Farm irrigation scheme.

Radcot Bridge

There are, in fact, three bridges over the river here - Pidnell Bridge, Canal Bridge and, what is claimed to be the oldest stone bridge on the Thames, Radcot Bridge. The latter was built of Taynton stone in around 1200 and had three pointed arches. According to a Saxon charter there has been a bridge here since 958. Cistercian monks of St Mary at Citeaux, in Normandy, were granted land for the bridge by King John. It became a toll bridge in 1312: *'a grant for pontage for 5 years, for the repair of the bridge, upon all wares for sale carried across'.* Much of the structure was broken down during the Battle of Radcot Bridge in 1387 and reconstructed six years later. It is said that the central arch was demolished to create a fish trap and then rebuilt. It was severely damaged again during the Wars of the Roses after which it was rebuilt with a flattened central arch.

Radcot Bridge was built over the river. But in 1787 a cut for the Severn & Thames Canal was dug across the bend in the river and this then became the main navigable channel. The original course was relegated to a backwater. A new, single arched bridge was built over the cut in 1798, at a cost of £400, which connected to the old bridge.

With Lechlade, the highest shipping point on the river, not far away the wharf at Radcot, next to the Swan pub, was commercially very important. It was a centre for the distribution of coal to local villages.

Radcot Cradle is a pedestrian timber bridge over the original main channel at the point where the canal cut leaves the river course. It was on the site of Monks Mill and fishery, recorded here in 1492, but pulled down in 1791. In 1731 it was stated that *'every boat or barge passing Old Eye (Monks Mill) shall pay 1d per ton'.*

Old Man's Bridge

Originally this was the site of a weir with a footpath over the top. It was an important crossing point linking several market towns on either side of the river. The weir had disappeared by 1868. A bridge was still standing there but it was in a poor state of repair. The weir piles were removed and a new footbridge built (also called High Bridge). By 1894 this steep trestle with five openings was unsafe and it was replaced by the present bridge.

Rushey Lock & Weir

The lock was built in stone in 1790 by the Thames Navigation Commission. The weir is adjacent to the lock on the other side of the lock island. The Thames Path crosses the river here by way of the lock gates and then across the weir itself. It was named after the rushes that grew here. In 1857 repairs were needed as it was *'in a most frightful state of dilapidation'* with only two gates out of four in operation and it was stuffed with hurdles and straw to keep the water up to a certain height. The weir was repaired in 1871 and the lock rebuilt in 1898.

Tadpole Bridge

The present bridge was built in stone with one large arch in 1796. An older bridge is shown on Robert Whitworth's 1784 map. Both were on the site of what has been named Tadpole Weir or Rudge's Weir or Kent's Weir. This weir was removed long after the bridge was built, in 1896. In 1877 there was a large coal wharf on the river here.

The Trout pub, restaurant and hotel is on the Oxfordshire side of the bridge. Thacker noted that at one time the legend over the door read *'The Trout, kept by A. Herring'*.

Thames Crossings 23

Tenfoot Bridge

This is a wooden footbridge built in 1869 on the site of a flash weir. The weir is mentioned in 1791, when ten feet of its paddles had to be removed to let vessels through. By 1869 the weir was in a very poor state of repair and needed replacing. As a right of way had long been established along its top, a timber footbridge was built in its place to continue the crossing. It may originally have been called Ten Bridge, a family name, or it may be a corruption of the river's name, Thames.

Shifford Lock Cut Bridge

This beam pound lock was initially constructed on its own in the middle of the fields and finished in 1897. Only then was the cut dug across the fields to incorporate the lock. A wooden footbridge crosses the cut and connects the villages of Chimney with Duxford. It was one of the last locks to be built on the Thames. Originally the river meandered south in a loop to Duxford Village and was crossed by the ford and a ferry.

Duxford Ford

The ford is still on the original course of the river and is now only navigable by canoe. Other vessels have to use the cut through to the lock. The ford links Duxford and Chimney villages. The Domesday Book records that the manor of Duxford, with a fishery and a watermill, was granted to William the Conqueror's half-brother, Odo, the Bishop of Bayeux. A ferry operated close to the ford. It stopped after the Shifford Lock Cut was opened in 1898 to control the flow of water past the village of Duxford.

New Bridge

New Bridge was built around 1250 by the monks of Deerhurst Priory which owned Northmoor, the manor of La Noe. Its purpose was to improve transport between wool towns in southern England and those in the Cotswolds. It is a stone built bridge with 12 spans and 5 piers in the water. In 1692 the bridge had 51 arches to carry the causeway and let flood waters pass when necessary. It was damaged in the Battle of New Bridge during the Civil War when Parliamentary troops tried, unsuccessfully, to cross the Thames to capture Charles by surrounding Oxford.

Today the bridge's structure is weakening, particularly in one arch, and traffic is limited to single file controlled by lights. There is a good pub/restaurant at each end – the Rose Revived on the north bank and the Maybush on the south bank.

Hart's Weir Footbridge

This cement footbridge was built in 1879 on the site of a weir. A right of way existed as a precarious crossing over the weir which was removed once the footbridge had been completed. The bridge crosses the river in a single, tall, arched span and the locals have named it Rainbow Bridge after this shape.

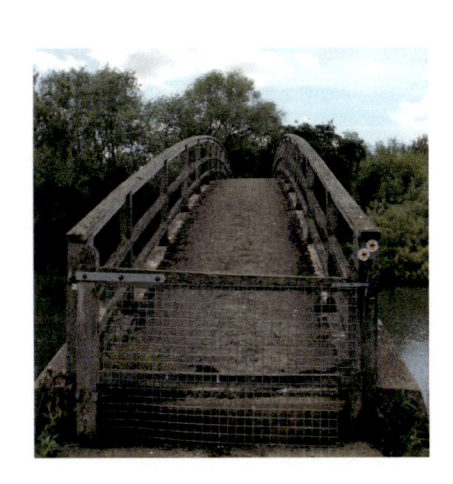

Bablock Hythe Ferry Crossing

The Ferry Man Inn, a stark, modernish building, contradictorily marks one of the most ancient crossing points of the Thames although the ferry itself was abandoned in the 1960's. The Romans are believed to have forded the river here. There is evidence of a ferry being here since 1279 when it was operated by John Cocas under a rental agreement with Deerhurst Priory. For much of its time it was used by Benedictine monks to travel between Eynsham Abbey, Northmoor Church, Abingdon Abbey and maybe as far as the White Horse Complex, Avebury Rings and Stonehenge. The ferry was a wide beamed punt operated by hauling on a rope or, later, a chain strung across the river. This was a hazard for vessels moving up and down the river. An ancient inn, the Chequers, was rebuilt in 1990's as the Ferry Inn. A caravan park now overlooks the site.

Pinkhill Lock & Weir

The river can be crossed here with public access across the upstream gate of the lock and then across the public walkway over the weir. The lock was built of stone and completed in 1791. It is on the site of a former weir and flash lock owned by Lord Harcourt. The lock was partially rebuilt in 1877. A cut had been dug below the lock by 1899.

Swinford Toll Bridge

The bridge at Swinford opened in 1769 as a privately owned toll bridge. It is a Georgian structure built of local limestone. It replaced an existing ferry and was funded by the Earl of Abingdon.

It is governed by its own Act of Parliament which allows the owner to collect tolls and makes it illegal to build other bridges up to three miles either side of it. The owners do not pay tax on the revenue.

In 1835 tolls for pedestrians and pedal cyclists were abolished. It was sold at auction in 2009 for £1.08 million. In 2016 the 10,000 cars that use the bridge every day are charged 5p to cross.

Eynsham Lock & Weir

The river can be crossed here by using the downstream lock gates and the walkway over the weir. A cut was dug across the neck of the large bend taken by the Thames and the lock was built in 1928 as one of the last pound locks on the river. There had been a flash lock and weir on the original river course for 6/700 years, known as Eynsham or Bolde's weir, and owned by Eynsham Abbey.

Wharf Stream runs to the north of the lock and the toll bridge. Its, yes, wharves, were used to load salt from Droitwich and stone from Burford, which had been bought here by horse and cart, onto barges for onward transport to Oxford and London. The weir was rebuilt in 1886 and four years later a boat slide was added to assist smaller craft in negotiating the fast flowing waters, and again in 1950.

The Thames around Wolvercote

At Wolvercote the Thames becomes a bit entangled. Wolvercote Mill Stream goes off on a big loop to the east before the Oxford bypass and then drops south to pass under Toll Bridge (now known as Airmen's Bridge) close to Wolvercote village and re-joins the main river south of the weir and lock. The Thames, itself, carries on under the A34 and passes the Trout Inn on the east bank with its narrow-arched timber bridge to its own private island. In the 18th century a lock cut was dug across the bend here to facilitate navigation.

Thames Bridge

This is a modern road bridge of concrete construction, completed in 1961 to carry the A34 and Oxford Ring Road. Just downstream from it an iron boundary marker displays the Oxford arms and the date,1886, marking the extent of the city of Oxford and the names of the mayor and the sheriff of Oxfordshire.

Godstow Bridge

Godstow bridge is in two parts. The older part, on the Wolvercote side, is built of stone and crosses the original course of the river near the Trout Inn. It was in existence in 1692. It has a pointed arch and dates from medieval times. It is thought that during the English Civil War, the Royalists held this bridge against the attacking Parliamentary army. Godstow Lock was constructed here in 1790 and another bridge was required to cross the newly dug lock cut to link with the old bridge. This new bridge was built in 1792 with two rounded arches of brick and was rebuilt in 1892.

The Ruins of Godstow Nunnery

The ruins of Godstow Abbey and Nunnery are situated on the west bank of the lock cut, downstream from the newer bridge. The complex was built in local limestone for Benedictine nuns in 1133. The abbey was enlarged in 1176 and again in 1188 when Henry II gave *"£258 (£100 for the church which was consecrated in 1159), 40,000 shingles, 4,000 lathes and much timber"*. At the time the abbey was the resting place of Rosamund Clifford, the long term mistress of the king. In 1539, under Henry VIII's 2nd Act of Dissolution, the abbey was suppressed and then destroyed, and with it, Rosamund's tomb. After the dissolution, George Owen converted the buildings into Godstow House, in which his family lived until 1645 when it was badly damaged during the Civil War. The locals then used its stone in the building of their own homes and outbuildings.

Wolvercote Paper Mill

The mill was in existence in 1720 and supplied paper to Oxford University. From 1782 it was leased to Oxford printer, William Jackson. It was water powered until 1811 when a steam engine was installed to power the paper making process. This engine used 100 tons of coal per week which was brought by barge down the Oxford Canal, then Dukes Cut and down the millstream to the mill. The mill was rebuilt in 1955. It ceased paper making in 1998 and was demolished in 2004.

The Trout Inn

The first building was built beside the river here in the 16th century. It was originally used by fishermen who leased the fishing rights from the Lords of Godstow and Wolvercote. It was probably an inn by 1625. Records show it was licenced by Oxford City Magistrates in 1707. It was entirely rebuilt in 1737 by the then tenant, Jeremiah Bishop. A timber bridge connects the pub to its own private island.

Toll Bridge, Wolvercote (Airmen's Bridge)

This is a former stone toll bridge built in 1876 over the millstream of Wolvercote Paper Mill. It is named after two airmen were killed in their monoplane as they came into land on Port Meadow, being used as an airfield during WW1. A wire came loose tearing a hole in their starboard wing. A plaque commemorates their death: *'In deep respect for the memory of Lieut. C.A. Bettington & Second-Lieut. E. Hotchkiss of the Royal Flying Corps who met their deaths in the wreck of a monoplane 100 yards north of this spot on Tuesday Sept 10 1912'.*

Thames Crossings 29

Port Meadow, Oxford

Port Meadow is the name of the open meadow that lines the east bank of the Thames from Wolvercote down to the edge of Oxford. It has been used as ancient grazing land for thousands of years and has never been ploughed. The 'town meadow' was presented to the burgesses of Oxford as 'free common' by William the Conqueror and recorded as such in the Domesday Book. Many fords crossed the river between Port Meadow and Binsey Green and were used by cattle, farm wagons, customers drinking at the Perch and pilgrims praying at Binsey church. The Binsey Boat was discovered in 2003, 20.6m long and 1m wide, with square ends - a typical, punt, horse-ferry boat, abandoned when the ferry service was discontinued. In the 17th century horse racing was held on the meadow, in WWI it was used as a military airfield and in WWII as a camp for Dunkirk evacuees.

Medley Footbridge

This is an iron footbridge on the edge of Oxford, painted red, which is known by locals as Rainbow Bridge due to its shape. In one span it joins the west bank of the river to Fiddler's Island and Port Meadow to the east. The word Medley signifies the 'middle island' in the river between the Osney bank and the Binsey bank. A plaque on the bridge states: *'This bridge was erected by public subs[c]ription through the exertion and during the shrievalty of Henry Grant Esquire AD 1865'*.

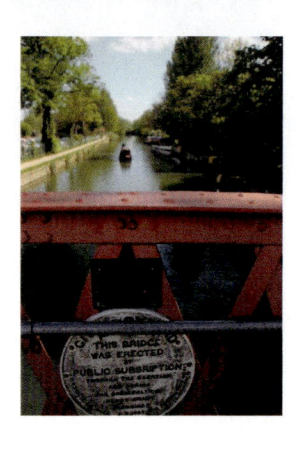

Osney Bridge

The original bridge was built by the monks of Osney Abbey to carry the main road across the millstream of the flour mill, which was located down Mill Street and now forms part of a new development of apartments on the island of Osney.

The abbey was founded in 1129 by Robert d'Oyley, one of William the Conqueror's knights. The Osney Cut was dug in 1227 and the Abbey accumulated great wealth both from charging tolls to river traffic and from the products from the mills lining the river and millstreams.

The miller in Chaucer's 'The Miller's Tale' was the miller of Osney Mill. The towpath crosses the river over Osney Bridge which has the lowest headroom of any bridge across the navigable Thames.

By the early 17th century the bridge was of stone construction with three arches. By the mid19th century it had become a serious obstruction to navigation and so when, in 1885, the central stone arch collapsed leaving a massive pier, it was replaced by an iron road bridge with a single span. This was completed in 1889.

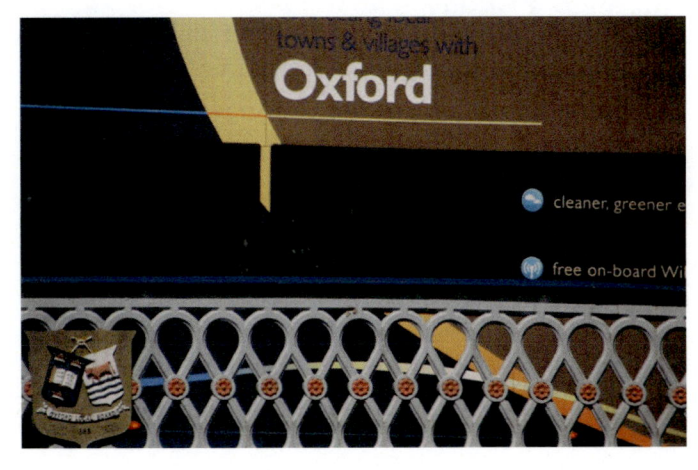

Osney Rail Bridge

This is single span iron bridge now carrying the Cherwell Valley Railway Line. It was built in 1850 to carry the Great Western Railway's new line from the original Oxford station at Grandpont to Rugby. A second bridge was built in 1887, within a metre of the original bridge.

Gasworks Bridge

The bridge was constructed by the Oxford & District Gas Company in 1886 for a short railway branch line to carry coal to the gas works on the north bank in St Ebbes. As St Ebbes grew there was only room to position the gas holders on the south bank and it was necessary to pipe the gas across the river. The bridge was constructed in iron with a brick plinth in the middle supporting the two spans. Sections were assembled on the river bank and floated into position. The Gasworks were demolished in 1960. The bridge is now used as a footbridge linking St Ebbes to Grandpont Nature Reserve, with the gas pipes underneath.

Grandpont Bridge

This is a single span footbridge made of iron girders and built in the 1930s to carry a utility pipe. A walkway was added in 1977. It now carries a footpath and a cycleway between Grandpont on the south bank and St Ebbes and the City Centre on the north.

Folly Bridge

This is a stone bridge designed by Ebenezer Perry and opened in 1827. The arched bridge crosses two channels of the river and an island, on which is situated the base for Salters Steamers and a castellated house, which may be the reason why the name 'Folly' was chosen for the bridge. The house was built in 1849 for the mathematician, Joshua Cardwell.

The bridge stands on the site of a ford over which oxen could be driven across the Isis, the reach between Folly Bridge and Iffley Lock - 'Oxenford'. There was a Saxon bridge here in the time of Ethelsed of Wessex. In 1025 the first known stone bridge over the river was built here by Robert d'Oyly, at the time Constable of Oxford Castle.

It was known as South Bridge until as late as the 17th century and formed part of a long causeway along Abingdon Road known as Grandpont ['the grand bridge' in French]. In 1369 there was a grant of pontage on 'Grauntpount'. It was said to be *'so dangerous as to be well-nigh impassable'*. Funds were required to build a new bridge and to maintain and repair it into the future. A toll gate was placed at the southern end of Abingdon Road to collect tolls for this purpose. In 1844 the toll house was moved onto the bridge itself, at a cost of £250. Tolls were abolished in 1850 and the gate was removed. The toll house first became a boat hire office and is now a shop.

The Island

On approaching the city along the causeway, down by the water on a narrow pontoon, an abandoned leather arm chair welcomes passers-by from the opposite bank to sit and contemplate the passing boats on the gentle current. Frustratingly, there is no way to reach it, unless you come from inside the castle keep. Abandoned supermarket trolleys would not be out of place here. On the town side, an elegant arrangement of white clothed tables, cloths and napkins face the bridge's arches and the spires of Oxford's colleges. This is much more welcoming on the riverside, as are its menu and its range of high menu wines. Now that is no folly.

The folly house on the island hides the thought of protruding cannons from its castellated roof. Saints and sinners gaze down from their enclaves as centuries of peasants and travellers arrive from the south in wagons and carts, excited at their arrival beneath the spires of the city. The rather sad toll booth now sells papers and chocolates and drinks to Chinese tourists, having abandoned its primary purpose beside the toll gate that has long been removed. Travellers still pay their few pence for refreshments and news after their long journey.

The Middle Reaches

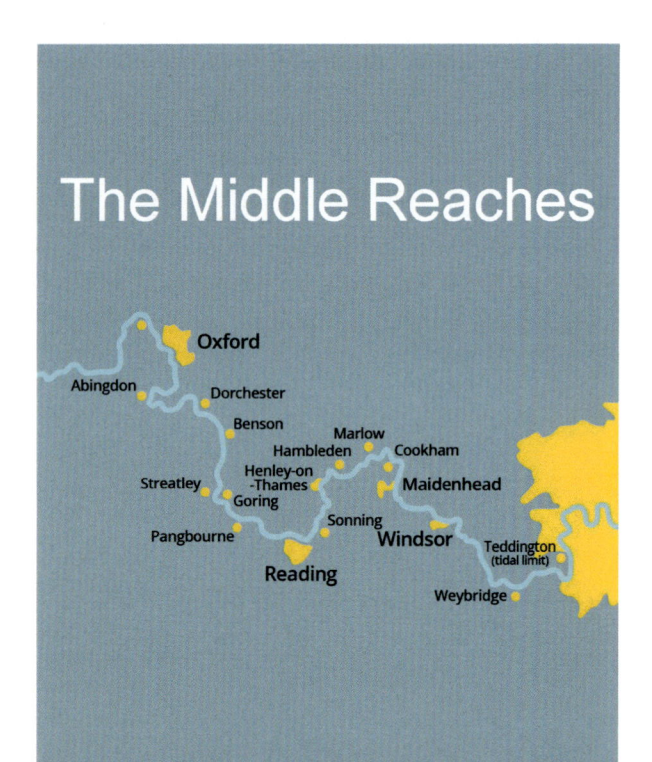

Oxford to Teddington

From Oxford, the Thames cuts south through the market towns and villages of the Thames Valley. The church spires of Abingdon and Wallingford stand proud reflecting past glories and present affluence. From here, it is south to the beer, bulbs and biscuits of Reading and then a long bend north through the towns of Henley-on-Thames and Marlow before wiggling southwards past Maidenhead, Windsor, Hampton Court and on through the last lock on the non-tidal river at Teddington. These settlements take full advantage of their riverside position to become political, economic and recreational centres, trading, milling, supplying, manufacturing, transporting to generate income, influence, power and wealth.

Crossing	Date
Donnington Bridge	1962
Iffley Lock & Weir	1793
Isis Road Bridge & Kennington Railway Bridge	1965 & 1923
Sandford Lock & Footbridge	1972
Nuneham Railway Bridge	1929
Abingdon Lock & Weir	1790
Abingdon Bridge	1422
Sutton Pool Weirs, Donkey Bridge & Sutton Bridge	1807/9
Appleford Railway Bridge	1844
Clifton Hampden Bridge	1867
Day's Lock & Weir & Little Wittenham Bridge	1789 & 1870
Shillingford Bridge	1827
Benson Lock & Weir	1870
Wallingford Bridge	1809
Winterbrook Bridge	1993
Moulsford Railway Bridge	1839
Goring & Streatley Bridge	1923
Gatehampton Railway Bridge	1838
Whitchurch Toll Bridge	1792
Cavershan Bridge	1927
Christchurch Bridge	2015
Reading Bridge	1923
Caversham Lock & Weir	1875
Sonning Bridge & Backwater Bridges	1775 & 1986
Shiplake Railway Bridge	1897
Henley Bridge	1786
Hambledon Lock & Weir	1884
Temple Footbridge	1989
Marlow Bridge & Marlow By-pass Bridge	1832 & 1972
Bourne End Railway Bridge & Walkway	1895
Cookham Bridge	1867
Maidenhead Bridge & Railway Bridge	1777 & 1839
M4 Thames Bridge	1960s
Summerleaze Footbridge	1996
Queen Elizabeth Bridge, Windsor	1966
Windsor Railway & Town Bridges	1849 & 1824
Victoria Bridge & Albert Bridge, Datchet	1967 & 1928
M25 & A30 Bridge, Runnymede	1961
Staines Bridge	1832
Staines Railway Bridge	1856
Chertsey Bridge	1785
Shepperton to Weybridge Ferry	C15th
Walton Bridge	2013
Hampton Ferry	1514
Hampton Court Bridge	1933
Kingston Bridge & Railway Bridge	1828 & 1863

Donnington Bridge

This is a modern road bridge constructed in reinforced concrete in a single arch and completed in 1962. There was a ferry here from the 14th century, alongside a ford which had existed from Roman times. The ferry ran as a free ferry and, in relatively recent times, it was still run by Oxford City Council until it was replaced by a concrete footbridge in 1937. The last ferryman was Thomas Rose, landlord of the Isis Public House. The Cementation Company was awarded the contract to build the road bridge and to demolish the free ferry and footbridge on completion.

Iffley Lock & Weir

Iffley, meaning 'on a little hill', is the first place down from Oxford from which river traffic could be surveyed and controlled and local people could live, safe from any floods. The site had been owned by Lincoln College from 1302 when there may have been a bridge of some kind.

The narrow bridge across the millstream forms the first element of the river crossing. Iffley mill was built here in the 12th century and bought by Lincoln College in 1445. It burned down in 1908. The mill was *'notorious for arguments between bargees and millers, who being in possession of the lock, flash or pound, could pressure the head of water and not let it flow down river by opening the gates as long as they wished'*. The mill ground malt, barley, corn and cereals. For a while in the 15th century it was a fulling mill (a step in making cloth which involves cleansing the wool to eliminate oils and make it thicker).

The pound lock was built in 1631. It was rebuilt in 1793 and the keeper instructed to take tolls for *'punts, pleasure boats, skiffs and wherries at a charge of sixpence for punts and skiffs and one shilling for four oared crafts'*. Access to the lock was awkward for barges heading upstream. These had to enter backwards and remove their masts. In 1826 it was ordered that no craft should pass through the lock during 'divine service'.

Once over the millstream there is a walkway over the bottom set of lock gates, and then a choice of two bridges at each end of the lock, one built in stone and the other in steel and wood. These cross a narrow channel where two sets of rollers help punts and rowing boats to move easily between the water levels without having to use the lock.

Thames Crossings 35

Isis Road Bridge

This is a modern road bridge built in a single steel arch in the 1960s. It was opened to traffic in 1965.

Kennington Railway Bridge

This steel bridge was built in 1923 for the Great Western Railway and replaced a wooden bridge that was first built in 1864. It now carries the freight railway branch line to BMW Mini factory at Cowley and joins the main line at Iffley Halt station (Kennington). This was opened in 1908 along with four other halts between Oxford and Wheatley. Services were provided by rail motors, a lightweight railcar with an integrated small steam unit or diesel/petrol engine. These were economic to build and were used on routes where passenger numbers were light. They were withdrawn in 1915 and the halts closed. The next station on the line into Oxford was Littlemore.

> From a distance, Kennington Railway Bridge seems to balance its girders on plinths across the river. Tall pylons stand on its arch bed as they applaud with outstretched hands. Close up, the paint peels, the purple thistles flourish, the weeds spread. The sound of diesels and carriages on the mainline suggest an approaching train but they shunter on in the distance leaving the bridge's skeleton alone and deserted. If you time it right you might, like a twitcher, catch a sighting of that rare, car-carrying train, transporting its cargo of 264 minis from the BMW factory to Purfleet in Essex for export to somewhere glam in the world. Five times a week these trains disturb the bird song and the peace and shake the bones of the old bridge. The rest is history.

Sandford Lock & Footbridge

The crossing here consists of a modern footbridge across the millstream, the bottom set of the present lock gates across the lock cut, and then a walk to one of two narrow bridges, both of which cross the western course of the river to the meadows beyond.

From way back when there has been a crossing across the river here using the islands between the Sandford and Kennington banks. The ancient river navigation channel took the western course, through Fiddler's Elbow and Sandford Pool to join up again with its other parts just south of the present lock. This is the site of an old ford with a lane and a causeway approaching the river from Sandford. On the western bank just below the lock, by the modern footbridge, is a mounting stone which would have been used by travellers to remount their horses having crossed the river on foot.

The Domesday Book counted 18 families living by this sandy ford. A ferry and a fish weir were recorded here in medieval times. In 1239 Sir Thomas de Sandford gave this land to the Knights Templars. Sandford ferry was a horse ferry and together with the mill, built in 1294, the fishery and the inn, run together as a single concern.

Where the river divides, stood the flash weirs, described in 1624 as 'Great Lockes'. Passage was always difficult and dangerous due to the process of having to remove paddles from the lock and having to either pull or haul boats through against the strong stream or riding the flash of water on the downstream journey. The flash lock was built for the benefit of the mill and enraged the bargemen of Oxford. In Edward III's time there is an account of such a conflict between millers and bargemen when *'the men of Oxon broke down the locks of Sandford'*.

A new pound lock was built on the eastern course. In 1632 after the miller had opened the sluices and damaged the bank, another lock was constructed in 1836, alongside the old one, which was then filled in.

In 1884 Henry and George Simmons, Reading Brewers, bought the rights to the buildings, the ferry, the tolls, the meadows and the mill. Tolls were payable *'in respect of all persons and all horses and cattle passing through and over the passage'*.

A new lock was opened on the present site in 1936 much of which was removed to build the present lock in 1972. The 2nd Wartime Boat Race was held here in 1943.

The pool below the main weir is known as the Sandford Lasher and has been notorious due to the number of people who drowned there. Within living memory there was a ferry and then a toll bridge at the Kings Arms, taking passengers and vehicles over the river.

Nuneham Railway Bridge

The railway bridge was built in 1929 and replaced an earlier wooden bridge built in 1844. It is an iron construction on a single brick plinth. Nearby is the site of the Radley Ferry which linked Nuneham Courtney to Radley from the 13th to 19th centuries.

Abingdon Lock & Weir

The original main stream of the Thames probably cut south, down Swift Ditch, missing the growing town of Abingdon. Between 955 and 963 the monks of Abingdon Abbey dug another channel to the west, closer to the town. Excavated further by Abbot Ordric in 1060, this remained the main channel for over 700 years although Swift Ditch was still faster as it cut due south to re-enter the Thames at the stone bridges of Culham. For the Abbey the river provided fish for non-meat eating days, power to drive mills and was a source of wealth through the payment of tolls by boats travelling to and from Oxford. There were frequent arguments between those who operated the fisheries and the millers who needed a good head of penned water to operate their mills. The release of water often damaged the fisheries.

In 1624 a pound lock was built at the top of Swift Ditch in an attempt to return the main channel to its original course. However, in 1790, to attract trade back to the town, Abingdon citizens built the present lock on their stretch of the river and Swift Ditch became a backwater. There were originally two weirs on the outskirts of Abingdon which enabled horses to cross the river with the tow path but now only one remains. The river can be crossed by using the walkway across this present weir and the bottom lock gates.

Abingdon Mill

The millstream, which branches off into the town at the present weir, was a project started by Abbot Ethelwold in 954AD. Its purpose was to provide drainage and remove sewage from the Abbey and power the abbey's fulling and corn mills, granary, bake house and brewhouse. The flow of water is regulated by the weir. In 1538 there were three corn mills under one roof where the Upper Reaches Hotel now stands. Fulling both removes grease, so cloth will later take dye, and felts it. The cloth was beaten while immersed in a mixture of clay, urine and soapy plant extracts. This process was mechanised by the 12th century and required water power. Cloth is passed through a trough of the mixture and then beaten within it with a set of shaped mallets ('stocks') which are raised and dropped by a camshaft attached to a water wheel. After fulling, the cloth was stretched and flattened on frames set out on the meadows.

Abingdon Bridge

Abingdon Bridge is, in fact, two bridges, linked by Nags Head Island in the middle of which, there is an excellent pub of the same name. Abingdon Bridge is the northern part nearest the town which has six arches and crosses the backwater and mill stream. The southern part is technically called Burford Bridge and has one main arch and four minor arches at the river and two minor arches on the floodplain

The Thames has been forded here, with difficulty, since 6/700BC. Prior to the 15th century both the river at Abingdon and Swift Ditch at Culham had to be crossed by ferry and drowning incidents were frequent. In 1416 a group of Abingdon merchants, led by Geoffrey Barbour and John Howchion, financed the crossings at Abingdon and Culham which were completed in 1422. Both were spanned by stone bridges and were linked by a causeway. In 1553 the Charity of Christ's Hospital was created to fund the burden of repairs to Abingdon's four bridges over the Thames and the Ock.

During the Civil War, drawbridges were inserted into all four of Abingdon bridges. In 1645, Royalist attacks over Culham Bridge were beaten off by the Parliamentary garrison. The bridge originally had 11 arches which were later extended to 14. In 1790 the bridge was partially rebuilt but the roadway was still too narrow for more than a single line of traffic. It was widened in 1829 and rebuilt in 1927 when three of the 15th century arches were demolished and replaced with one span to aid navigation.

Swan Upping dates from medieval times when swans were valued as a delicacy at banquets and feasts. Today, the Crown retains the right to own all unmarked mute swans on certain stretches of the river. Ownership is shared with the Vintners' and Dyers' Companies, who were both granted rights in the 15th century. Each year, six traditional Thames rowing skiffs, manned by Swan Uppers and headed by The Queen's Swan Marker, journey upstream as far as Abingdon. The Swan Uppers weigh, measure and ring any cygnets they find but leave unmarked the young of any Crown swans.

Sutton Pool Weirs

At this point the river takes a long bend down through the village of Sutton Courtenay which, in the past, had a number of weirs and locks to power its mills. The Domesday Book records a mill on the Thames at Sutton Pools or Sudton (South Town, a town to the south of Abingdon) and in 1086 it contained three mills and 300 acres of river meadows. The mill stream and causeway were constructed, probably by local serf labour, between 950 and 1000 AD.

In 1697 the Bank of England required a special paper for printing its banknotes and Thomas Napper of Sutton Mill was awarded the contract. The mill itself was closed in 1897. The river used to pass underneath the paper mill until it was demolished. This route is now blocked by a fence and the river disappears underneath and through the gardens of the mill house to reappear above Sutton Bridge.

A causeway stretches from the village into and across the river with a walkway across the top of a number of weirs. The original locks of Sutton Courtenay were inconvenient, expensive and unpopular. Boats were allowed to pass the mills but millers charged high tolls.

In 1809, to improve navigation, a cut was dug across the top of the bend and a new pound lock constructed. The new lock cut enabled river traffic to avoid these charges. It became the main navigable channel, rejoining the Thames just below the village at Sutton Bridge.

Culham Cut 'Donkey' Bridge

When the lock cut was dug, an arched timber bridge was constructed at the top end to extend the path over the Sutton Pool islands and weirs to link Sutton Courtney and Culham. Local folklore tells of a donkey which was regularly seen crossing this pedestrian bridge.

Sutton Bridge

Sutton Bridge was built over the main river channel in 1807 and replaced an earlier multi-arched bridge over the original weir. There was also a ferry here. Originally it was a toll bridge for traffic travelling between Culham and Sutton Courtenay. The bridge was built of stone with three arches over the river and two smaller ones over the floodplain. In 1809 a single arched extension was built over Culham Cut just below the lock.

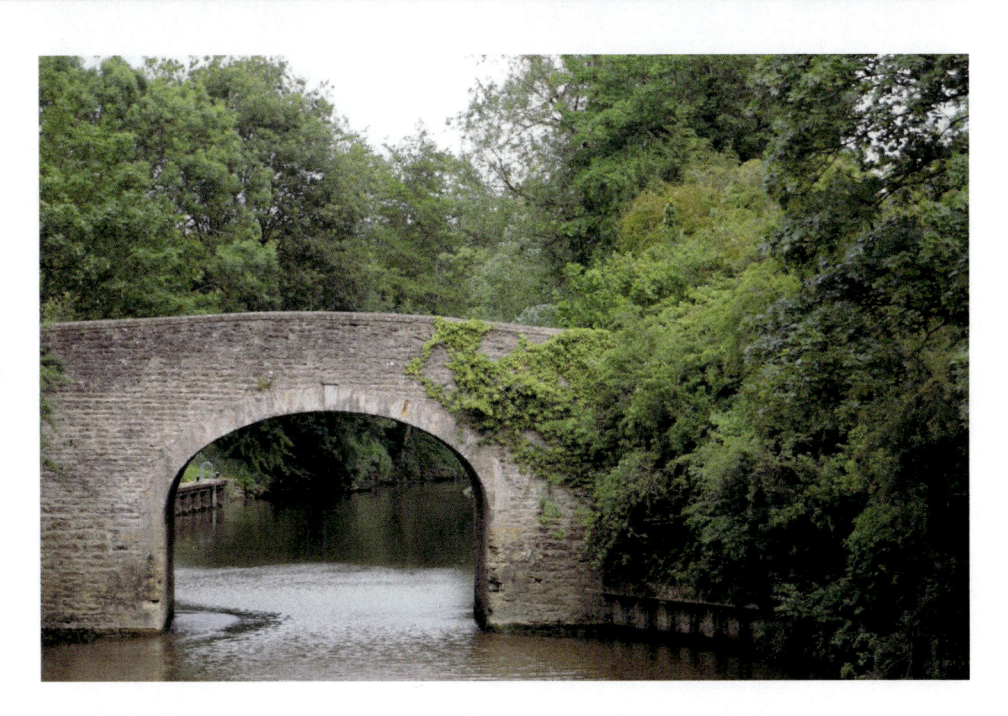

Thames Crossings 41

Appleford Railway Bridge

This is a bow and string iron bridge which opened in 1844.

Clifton Hampden Bridge

There had been a ferry here since the early 14th century when John Broun is mentioned as being the ferryman. In 1493 a Watlington draper, Roger Roper, gave Clifton Ferry to Exeter College, Oxford for carrying horses and men. The rights were sold to Henry Hucks Gibbs, Governor of the Bank of England in 1861. He had inherited Clifton Hampden Manor on the death of his father in 1842 and went about modernising the estate. He applied to Parliament for permission to build a bridge for public use. An Act of Parliament in 1864 stated 'the local and public advantage' of linking Clifton Hampden and Long Wittenham with a bridge. When it opened in 1867 its builder, Richard Casey, was the first toll keeper and no one else was allowed to operate a ford or a ferry within 200 yards of the bridge, the only exception being for towing horses. It has six brick spans with five piers in the water and triangular cutwaters which extend upwards to provide pedestrian refuges.

Day's Lock & Weir, Little Wittenham

The crossing at Day's Lock consists of the top gate of the lock and the walkway along the weir which goes straight across the river to the other side of Lock Island. The first pound lock was built here in 1789 on the site of a flash weir. It was staked out in 1788 when the weir owner had to remove his eel traps. In 1865 it was reported to be an *'utter ruin and dangerous'* but it was not repaired until 1871. The present lock was built in 1923. It is the main gauging station for the measurement of the water flow in the Thames.

Little Wittenham Bridge

This is a footbridge spanning the river in two parts with the Lock House Island in between. The bridge that connects Wittenham to the island is a flat steel structure on pillars with a metal guard. The other bridge connects the island to the Dorchester side and is arched and made of iron and wood. This latter bridge is used for the World Pooh Sticks Championships every summer.

In 1839 there were two ferries at this point. Wittenham Ferry crossed where the bridges were constructed with the ferryman living on the island. This was on the site of a ford which allowed movement between Wittenham Clumps, on the Sinodun Hills, and Dorchester. When the river was high and crossing became difficult, another ferry crossed upstream on the site of the weir at Day's Lock.

Shillingford Bridge

This is a stonebuilt road bridge dating from 1827. It is on the site of an early ferry called Keen Edge (Cane Hedge), a reference to the osier beds along the river bank. This, in turn, was on the site of a ford. In the Patent Rolls of 1301 the Earl of Cornwall is recorded as leasing a fishery *'downstream from Shillingford Bridge'*. Thacker dates its original construction to 957.

The medieval bridge was dismantled by 1379 when Shillingford Ferry was granted for life to Roger Hurst, porter of Wallingford Castle. The ferry remained a benefit to the castle's porter until 1530 when it was leased to Roger Hacheman for 33s 4d per annum. He also leased a small dwelling on the south bank in 1545. which was expanded several times and was known as the Swan Inn (now called the Shillingford Bridge Hotel).

Thomas Baskerville's travel journal of 1692 reports *'At Shillingford a great barge to waft over carts, coaches, horse and man'*. An Act of Parliament was passed in December 1763 to *'repair and widen the road from Shillingford through Wallingford to Pangbourne and Reading and to build a bridge over the Thames at or near Shillingford Ferry'*. The ferry was described as dangerous to use in times of flood. The Shillingford to Reading Turnpike Trust was created in 1764 to carry out the work. The Trust took a loan of £7,700 to purchase the ferry rights, construct the bridge and erect the toll gate on the bridge to collect tolls. The work started in 1766 with the building of stone foundations, piers and abatements to support a wooden trestle road and was completed one year later.

By 1826 this bridge was in poor repair. It was closed and a ferry provided while a new stone bridge was built. This required another Act of Parliament which laid down a fine of 20/40 shillings *'for any person who shall not keep his carriage on the left side of the road'*. A toll keeper's cottage was built on the downstream side on the north bank. In response to competition from The Reading to Oxford Railway, which opened in 1844, the bridge was passed to Berkshire and Oxfordshire County Councils. In 1852 under renewed powers, additional tolls were allowed for vehicles *'drawn by steam or machinery'*. In 1874 tolls were abolished.

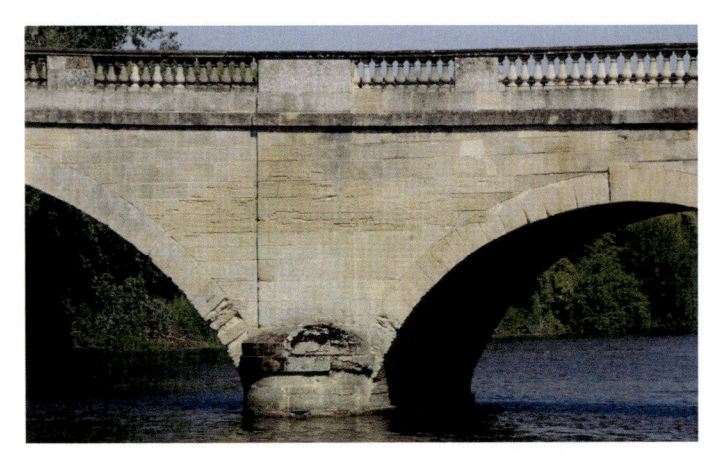

Benson Lock & Weir

The present lock was built in masonry in 1870 on the site of a weir, a flash lock and a ferry. The history of the weir can be traced back into the late 14th century when there was a mill at 'Bensington'. The first reference to the flash lock was in 1746. This was replaced by the first pound lock in 1788.

The ferry was still operating at this time and it is recorded, again in 1788, that '*a ferry line for Benson Ferry cost £1 10s 6d, a punt pole cost 1s 6d and Joseph Ashby was lock keeper and the ferryman, earning £15 12s per annum*'. The ferry stopped when the weir walkway and the lock gates were opened to allow the general public to cross the river at this point.

Wallingford Bridge

This is an arched bridge, built out of stone, with 22 spans of varying sizes, dating from the mid 13th century. It has been repaired on several occasions since then. William the Conqueror's army either forded or was ferried across the river here in 1066. Wallingford was the lowest point of the river which could be forded reliably, all year round. Reference is made to a, probably timber, bridge here in 1141 when King Stephen besieged Wallingford Castle.

In 1571 Elizabeth I allowed tolls to be charged for going over and passing under the bridge. During the siege of Wallingford Castle, in 1646, four arches were removed and a drawbridge inserted. The arches were replaced with timber structures which remained until 1751 when bricks and stone facing were used. In 1671 wardens were placed on the bridge to prevent plague victims from Crowmarsh entering the town.

After a flood, which took away three arches, the bridge was largely rebuilt in 1809, with a balustrade and a parapet. In 1819 a toll house was opened on the bridge on the large abutment on the paddling pool side. The toll gate was removed in 1881.

Crowmarsh Ferry operated at this point until it eventually fell into disuse in 1914 still charging a 1/2d toll.

There was another official ferry a few hundred metres downstream from the bridge at Chalmore Hole, set up in 1787 when the Thames Conservancy first put in the tow path. It carried horses from one bank to the other at a cost of 2d. Bargees would unharness their horses, put them on the ferry and re-attach them on the other side. Ferry House still exists as a private dwelling. The ferry crossed to Newnham Murren, a tiny village on the Oxfordshire side. The last ferry crossed in 1953. In 1838 a lock & weir were built across the river here to raise water levels in the summer. Much of the weir was damaged by floating ice in 1881 and the lock was completely removed two years later.

Winterbrook Bridge

This modern road bridge was built as part of the by-pass around Wallingford and opened in 1993. It is constructed of concrete and steel in three spans with reinforced plastic cladding on the underside. Grimms Ditch, the Iron Age earthworks that protects southern Oxfordshire, comes down to the river here through Mongewell Park and a ford or ferry would have existed in the past.

Moulsford Railway Bridge

The building of the first original bridge began in 1838. It was designed by Isambard Kingdom Brunel for the Great Western Railway to carry two broad gauge tracks. It is constructed from red bricks with four elliptical skew arches across the river. In 1892 broad gauge was dispensed with and the line was converted to take four tracks of standard gauge. A second, narrower bridge was built parallel to the original with the same profile and dimensions to take two of these tracks. The inside of the bridges can be reached through inspection doors to access the hollow space that runs all the way through, designed to reduce the weight of bricks on each arch.

On this stretch of the river a number of ferries existed, plying between the Oxfordshire and Berkshire banks:

- The North Stoke Ferry was used for hay and corn wains to get to fields on the Berkshire side. It was out of use by 1894 when a reference is made to the ferry being found at the bottom of a deep pool opposite the church

- Up to at least 1920 Little Stoke Ferry crossed the river to enable locals to reach Cholsey

- The Beetle and Wedge Ferry, also known as Moulsford Ferry, crossed to the village of South Stoke. The Beetle and Wedge, on the Berkshire side, is now a restaurant, a bar and a bed & breakfast

- The Leatherne and Bottel Ferry ferried customers from the opposite tow path. The restaurant and bar remains on the Oxfordshire bank

Goring & Streatley Bridge

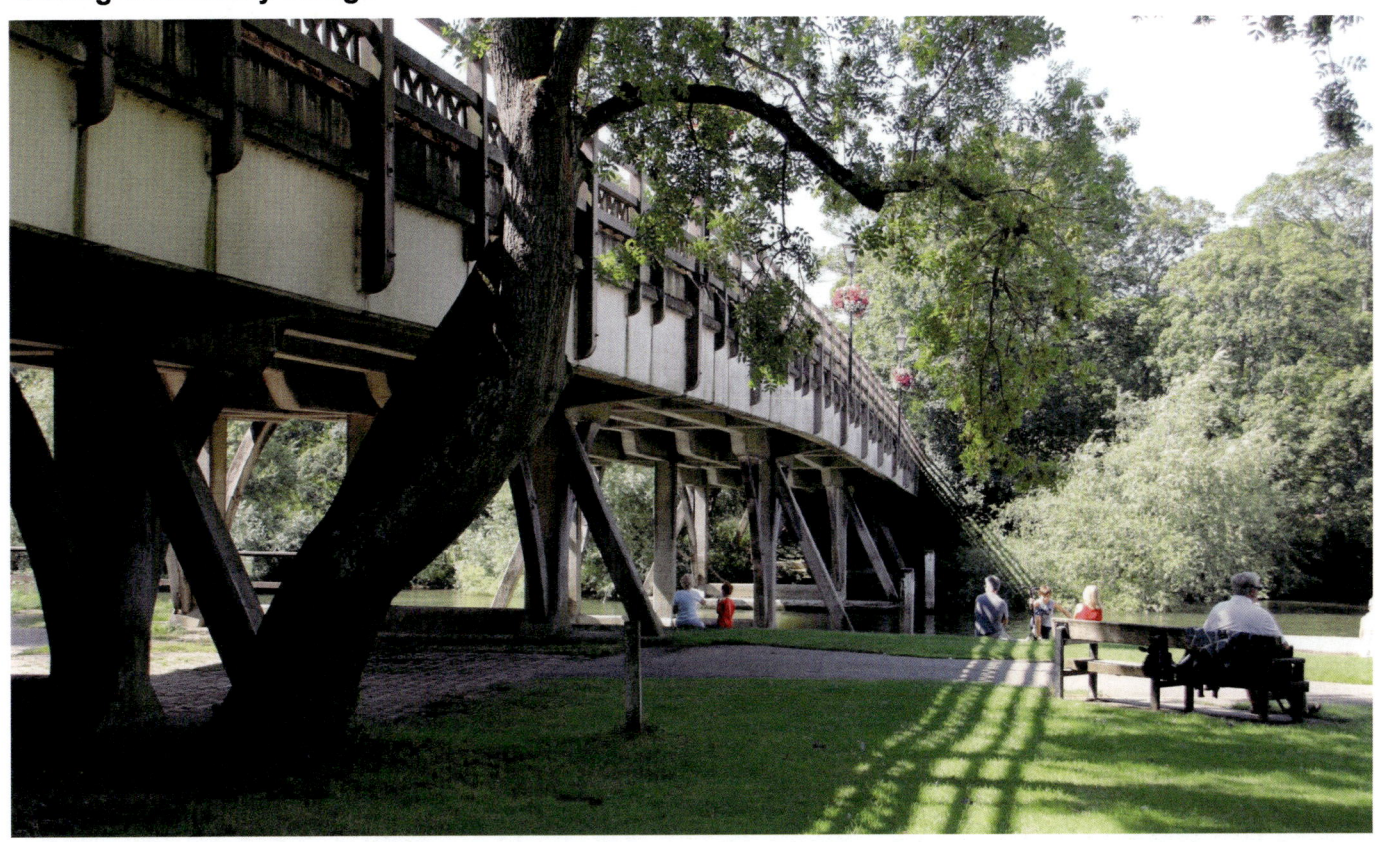

A new road bridge, made with timber struts supporting a metal roadway, was built here in 1923. It links Goring-on-Thames (Oxfordshire) and Streatley (Berkshire) over an island in the middle of the river. There has been a river crossing point here for 10,000 years, from before Britain was an island. The long distance paths, the Ridgeway and the Icknield Way, meet here and they both cross the Thames at this point, known as the Goring Gap.

This is the site of one of the oldest, and most picturesque, locks on the river. By Henry VIII's time there was a flash lock and a weir here. It was also the site of a ferry. In 1674, after partying at the Goring Feast, 60 residents of Berkshire drowned when the ferry capsized on their return to Streatley. In 1837 a wooden toll bridge was built to replace the ferry and this, in turn, was replaced by the present bridge. In 1837 tolls were set at:

For every horse mule or other beast drawing any coach stage coach chariot landau barouche sociable hearse litter break curricle with four wheels drawn by more than one horse	3d
For every dog drawing any cart truck or other such carriage	2d
For every carriage moved or propelled by steam, or other power other than animal power, for each wheel	1/-

Gatehampton Railway Bridge

Built by Brunel in 1838 as part of the Great Western mainline it was widened in 1892. It is made of brick to an arched design with two piers in the water. It is situated just above the site of a flash weir, which was in operation in 1402.

Whitchurch Toll Bridge

The Original Company of Proprietors of Whitchurch Bridge own and maintain this private toll bridge. It was built in 1792 where there had existed a ferry. The original charges were *'a halfpenny each for pedestrians, sheep, boar, pigs and 2 pence for each and every wheel of a carriage'*. The present toll (2016) is 60p for cars. It is maintained entirely from toll receipts. The structure was renewed in 1852 and again in 1902 and in 2014. This latest reconstruction was completed with new, stronger pilings and steel spans. The white lattice iron girders from the 1902 structure were taken away and refurbished and then incorporated into the new design.

Reading Festival Footbridge

This was first erected in 2008 (the festival started in 1998). It is craned into position to link campsites and car parking on the Mapledurham bank to the festival site itself. It is placed on permanent footings set on either side of the river on the bank. It is only for use by festival goers. Each year it is dismantled, stored and erected again for the following festival. It replaced a previous ferry service for festival goers which had long queues to get across.

Caversham Bridge

In 1927 the new Caversham Bridge, built in concrete with granite balustrades, was opened.

The first mention of a bridge here was 1231 - *'the chapel of St Anne on the bridge at Reading'*. In the same year, rather surprisingly, an oak was granted from Windsor Forest for a boat to ferry *'poor folk over Caversham Water'*. In 1480 *'the people of Reading complained to Edward IV of the abbot's negligence in repairing a part of the Caversham Bridge.* In 1530 Leland wrote: *'a great mayne bridge of tymbre over the Tamise, most upon foundation of Tymbre and yr sum places stone'*.

In 1644 a drawbridge was suggested, fit for carriages to pass. Some rebuilding took place in 1747. However, by 1812 the whole structure was in ruin and, following a fatality, some more rebuilding was required. In 1830 a new bridge was built.

By 1847, the Oxfordshire part was an old fashioned stone and brick structure and the Berkshire part a sort of makeshift wood and iron skeleton. In 1869 an iron bridge was *'thrown across'* the river, divided in the centre by Piper's Island, *'upon which stands an inn'*, which was replaced by the present bridge.

Christchurch Bridge

This pedestrian and cycle bridge was completed in 2015 to link Caversham and Reading's new railway station. It is supported by steel cables suspended from a 37m high mast.

Reading Bridge

Reading Bridge was opened in 1923 with a single arch across the river and with balustrades made of concrete. Plans for a bridge had been drawn up in 1912 but postponed due to the war. Previously there was no bridge on this site. It was decided to build a new bridge here as part of a political accommodation when Reading absorbed the village of Caversham. Once Reading Bridge was built, Caversham Bridge was, in turn, demolished and rebuilt.

Caversham Lock & Weir

The original pound lock was built in 1778 and rebuilt in 1875. The lock and weir connect to Lock Island and then a walkway connects to a weir complex, Verdant View Island and Heron Island, to act as another crossing over the river in the space of less than a mile. In 1493 a weir, a mill, a flash lock and a ferry were all present at this site.

Sonning Bridge

This narrow brick bridge with its 11 arches was completed in 1775. Traffic lights now restrict traffic to one-way due to its width. A timber bridge is mentioned here in Saxon times in 1125. It is not till 1530 that a definite reference is made to a timber bridge at Sonning which was rebuilt in 1567. Throughout the 17th Century there are reports of the bridge being in a state of decay and in need of repair. There is a stone at the centre of the bridge marking the county line between Berkshire and Oxfordshire which was also the ancient border between Mercia and Wessex.

Sonning Backwater Bridges

These two, flat bridges were rebuilt in 1986. There was a rickety, wooden structure here across the mill race and Sonning Backwater, linking the brick bridge with the smaller hamlet of Sonning Eye. This was replaced with a steel and iron structure in 1902. Downstream, a wooden pedestrian bridge crosses over to the other bank.

P H Ditchfield wrote in Vanishing Britain in 1910

The passing away of the old bridges is a deplorable feature of vanishing England. Since the introduction of those terrible traction-engines, monstrous machines that drag behind them a whole train of heavily laden trucks, few of these old structures that have survived centuries of ordinary use are safe from destruction. The immense weight of these road-trains are enough to break the back of any of the old-fashioned bridges. Constantly notices have to be set up stating: "This bridge is only sufficient to carry the ordinary traffic of the district, and traction-engines are not allowed to proceed over it". Then comes an outcry from the proprietors of locomotives demanding bridges suitable for their convenience. County councils and district councils are worried by their importunities, and soon the venerable structures are doomed, and an iron-girder bridge hideous in every particular replaces one of the most beautiful features of our village.

When the Sonning bridges that span the Thames were threatened a few years ago, English artists, such as Mr. Leslie and Mr. Holman-Hunt, strove manfully for their defence. The latter wrote:--

'With regard to the three Sonning bridges, parts of them have been already rebuilt with iron fittings in recent years, and no disinterested reasonable person can see why they could not be easily made sufficient to carry all existing traffic. If the bridges were to be widened in the service of some disproportionate vehicles it is obvious that the traffic such enlarged bridges are intended to carry would be put forward as an argument for demolishing the exquisite old bridge over the main river which is the glory of this exceptionally picturesque village'.

Shiplake Railway Bridge

Shiplake Railway Bridge was built in iron and opened in 1897. It had two twin river spans of wrought iron plate girders supported in the centre of the river on a pair of cast iron cylinders filled with concrete. It replaced an earlier timber bridge built for the Great Western Railway in 1857.

In 1881 George Leslie wrote:

'The railway bridge being of wood is by no means an eyesore on the river, but I do not think it a very safe one in a winter flood, in passing under it at which times it seems as if the weight of water must carry it away, and if any large piece of the weir or lock were to give way, and drifting down, strike on the timbers of the bridge at the time a train was passing across, I would not give much for the chance of escape of its passengers. I think one or two piles placed as outposts to the piers on the upper side, would very likely break the force of the blow, and might save the bridge; it is the nearness of the weir and lock to the bridge which suggests the likelihood of such a mishap'.

In 1889 A S Krausse, in his Pictorial History of the Thames, wrote:

'Immediately below Shiplake Lock, and just past the entrance to the River Loddon, the stream is crossed by one of the most hideous railway bridges in existence. It is a wooden structure, and has the appearance of tottering senility, its narrow arches being a veritable danger to all who pass under them'.

In the 1970s the line was reduced to a single track and the downstream side of the twin span was removed, leaving the brick abutments and central cast iron pier still in place.

Henley Bridge

The present bridge was built in Headington stone with five elliptical arches over the water and completed in 1786. It was built alongside the old timber bridge which was 'decayed and ruinous'.

In 1985 the earliest remains of two 2 stone arches were excavated – one on the Berkshire side and one in the cellar of the Angel Inn on the Oxfordshire side. Both date back to the late 12th Century. A bridge existed here by 1225 when the king granted custody of it 'at pleasure'. In 1232 it is stated in the Patent Rolls that 'the keeper of the bridge at Henley is to get his timber toll free from Windsor Forest'. In 1354 there were two granaries on the bridge.

By 1587 houses had been built on the bridge, described by Camden in 1610 as 'a timber bridge'. In 1645 £50 was charged to the inhabitants of the town after the bridge had been broken down by military forces during the Civil War.

The timber part was rebuilt in 1719 although it remained unstable and was repeatedly damaged by floods. In 1754 major repairs were required and Henley corporation provided a ferry. 15 years later Sambroke Freeman of Fawley Court arranged for the structure of the old bridge to be covered with boards to represent a bridge in Florence. A great flood swept it away in 1774. It was repaired but remained in a perilous state.

An Act of Parliament was passed in 1781 authorising a new Henley Bridge and in 1784/5 the old bridge was demolished. The new bridge was built along the north side of the old one. The keystone of the central arch on each side of the bridge displays sculptures of Isis and Tamesis by Anne Seymour Damer.

The first Oxford and Cambridge Boat Race finished here in 1829. Henley Regatta takes place every year over the first weekend in July, attracting crews from all over the world.

Hambledon Lock & Weir

The crossing here is rather glorious, consisting of the long walkway across the weir into the middle of the river and then taking a dog-leg that leads to the lock and over that gate to the other bank. The lock was rebuilt in 2000.

The mill and weir are mentioned in the Domesday Book. The weir is mentioned again in 1338 as having a winch for pulling boats through the flash lock. An inquest into the death of Wyllos and Robert Asshde in the 1380s stated that with others they '*were hauling a vessel up the weir with two cables and were killed through the lines parting and striking them so violently that their heads were broken*'.

A pound lock with a long weir was built in 1773. Caleb Gould was appointed in 1777 as the first lock keeper. He baked bread for the bargemen, he ate a dish of onion porridge every night, wore a long coat with many buttons and walked to Hambledon every day. He died in 1836 at the age of 92 having been in post for 59 years.

By 1814 the lock was dilapidated and in danger of collapse. It was entirely rebuilt in 1870 by George Leslie. In 1890 the lock keeper Charles Phillis was drowned in the lock. He couldn't swim. At the time the Thames Conservancy charged three pence for passing through the lock.

In 1884 the new weirs were constructed and then, following public complaints, the walkway was built to reopen an ancient right of way over the river.

In 1829 the lock was the start of the first University Boat Race. The course ended at Henley Bridge. Oxford won in a time of 14 minutes and 30 seconds.

Temple Footbridge

This pedestrian bridge was built in 1989 to take the Thames Path back across the river to the north bank. At 88 yards it is the longest hardwood bridge in the UK. In 1773 there was a ferry here, just above Temple Lock, which crossed the river so bargees could change their towing horses to the towpath on the other side. The ferry ceased operation in 1953.

The area's name of Temple Mill Island is derived from the Knights Templar who owned it, the mill and the surrounding islands. The mill was originally built as a flour mill and changed to a copper foundry in 1710 when the Thames and Severn Canal opened, enabling copper to be carried in barges from Swansea. The island once had three water mills for beating copper and brass into pots, pans and kettles. Daniel Defoe describes, in 1748, the making of thimbles: *'cast brass into large broad plates and they beat them out by force of great hammers wrought by the water mill into what shapes they might think fit to sell'*. The last mill closed in 1969.

Marlow Bridge

Marlow Bridge was built between 1829 and 1832 to replace the wooden bridge sited further downstream which eventually collapsed in 1833 due to the growing traffic on the Reading and Hatfield Turnpikes. In the 1950s it was proposed to replace the suspension bridge with a ferro-concrete span. This was vigorously opposed and in 1965 the suspension bridge was reconstructed.

The main span is 255 feet long, now with a weight limit of 3 tonnes, which is imposed by the use of traffic signals to restrict heavy traffic to single file. Tierney Clark was appointed to design and supervise the construction in 1829. He also designed Hammersmith, Shoreham and the Széchenyi Chain Bridge which spans the River Danube in Budapest and is a larger scale version of Marlow bridge. It is the only suspension bridge across the non-tidal Thames.

It is said that there was a bridge at Marlow as early as 1227. The Knights Templar of Bisham owned a bridge here in 1309. Gilbert de Clare, Earl of Gloucester and Hertford was given permission to raise funds for the repair of *'your bridge which is decayed and broken'*. For four years he could take a penny toll for all vessels *'that passed under the bridge laden with goods of value exceeding 40 shillings'*. In 1353 the toll charged had risen to 3d.

Leland stated in 1530 that it was *'a bridge made of timbre'*. Parliamentary forces partly destroyed it in 1642. A new timber bridge was built by public subscription in 1789, with the Thames Navigation Commission contributing £50 to raise the headroom by 18 inches following complaints from barge masters that the old bridge's *'navigable arch'* was too low and *'greatly impedes navigation'*.

Marlow By-pass Bridge

This road bridge was built in 1972 and carries the A404 which links the M4 and the M40. There is no crossing for pedestrians. It is made of concrete, with three spans across the river and the flood plain.

Bourne End Railway Bridge & Walkway

It was originally a timber bridge designed by Isambard Kingdom Brunel and his successor T. Bartram which opened in 1857 as part of the Wycombe Railway. It carried the Marlow branch line over the river. This service was called the Marlow Donkey although it is unclear how it got this name.

The narrow spans were unpopular with river traffic and it was reconstructed in steel in 1895. A latticed footbridge was added in 1992 which cantilevers out from the railway bridge. In 2013 the bridge was restored and repainted green. Hundreds of rivets that had almost rusted away were replaced.

There is still evidence of Spade Oak Ferry on Bourne End waterfront. This operated across the river from 1822.

Cookham Bridge

The present iron bridge dates from 1867. There has been a settlement at Cookham for many thousands of years. The first recorded river crossing here was where the Camlet Way, a Roman road, crossed the river at Hedsore Wharf. The remains of a Roman bridge have been discovered at this spot. When the Romans left, the bridge fell into disrepair and a number of ferry sites were established. These ferries formed part of the Great West Road until Maidenhead Bridge was constructed in 1280.

It was not until 1836 that the Cookham Bridge Company (CBC) invited proposals for a fixed crossing. Isambard Kingdom Brunel submitted designs for a cast iron suspension bridge at an estimated cost of £20,000 but this was not accepted as it was so costly. The CBC chose a design of George Treacher for a wooden bridge at an estimated cost of £2,000. Parliament gave approval to charge tolls on the new bridge and shares were issued. The CBC then bought the ferry rights at the site from Mr Poulton for £2,275 which included *'one barge with chains and rollers for the carriage of cattle and one punt with poles for the conveyance of passengers'*. The ferry was rented to John Beasley for £2 4s 3d per month to provide a service over the river while the bridge was being built.

In May 1839 a Mr Freebody was contracted to construct the wooden bridge. It had 13 spans and opened in January 1840. It was rented out to Mr Bolton at an annual rent of £350 although by 1844 it only produced £330 per annum in tolls. The following years saw a deterioration in the condition of the bridge due to its wooden construction. In 1859 the Cookham Bridge Company was informed that several of the piles were *'very much decayed and not unlikely to give way'* and in 1864 that it *'may subside if a heavy vehicle passes over it'*. By 1865 only half a bridge remained and a vehicle ferry was used in its place. A year later the leasee asked for a reduction in rent as the toll incomes had fallen due to people being too afraid to use the bridge.

In 1866 the Cookham Bridge Company organised the construction of a new bridge of two wrought iron girders supported by eight pairs of concrete filled pillars. The estimated cost was £2,520 which was £1,000 cheaper than the estimate for the timber bridge in 1840. It was known as the *'cheapest bridge on the river for its size'*. Work started in 1866 and it was completed the following year. At that time the old bridge was demolished and the approaches rerouted to meet up with the new iron bridge.

Maidenhead Bridge

This is an arched bridge with thirteen spans which opened in 1777. The seven central arches are built of Portland stone and the three at each end are built of brick. Five piers are in the river.

The first bridge at Maidenhead was built of wood in 1280. The Great West Road was diverted to it and away from the ford at Cookham. A wharf was built next to the bridge and the area became known as Maidenhythe (New Wharf). In 1297 a grant of portage (tolls on traffic passing across and beneath it) was awarded to pay for repairs and for the construction of a new bridge. In 1337 the toll for a loaded barge to pass under, or for a cart to pass over the bridge, was 1d. Chapels were built on the approaches to the bridge to facilitate prayers or to give thanks for safe passage over the bridge and to collect tolls.

In the reign of Henry VII it was so unsafe that most travellers preferred to use the ferry. Maidenhead Guild was formed in 1452, to levy tolls and hold markets to raise funds to repair it.

During the Civil War, the bridge fell into disrepair and by 1660 it was in a perilous state. The bridge wardens petitioned Charles II in 1672 but had to wait seven years before a warrant for twenty oaks was issued for repairs. The corporation then complained to the Lord Treasurer, in 1714, about the poor quality of the trees. A further eighteen years passed before the treasury granted a warrant for 23 oaks. In 1750 the bridge was again in a bad state and a contract was awarded to carry out repairs at a cost of £794 9s 2d.

Rather than keep paying out to maintain the bridge, the town corporation decided to apply to Parliament to build a new toll bridge. This was authorised in 1771 although the commencement of work was delayed until a ferry had been put in place for use during construction. The foundation stone was laid in 1772. There followed delays for ice, frost and flooding but the central pier was eventually completed in 1775 and the bridge opened to traffic two years later.

Tolls were abolished in 1903 when the town corporation was taken to court for spending toll money on things other than bridge repairs. A large crowd gathered to remove the toll gates and throw them into the river. At the time the charge for a coach and horses was 1/-, for a motor car was 6d and for twenty sheep was 10d.

Maidenhead Railway Bridge

This is one of Isambard Kingdom Brunel's brick, arched bridges, constructed for the Great Western Railway and opened in 1839 with two spans across the river. At the time the brick arches were the flattest and widest in the world. Brunel wanted a gentle gradient to avoid a 'hump'. The flat arches were loaded with concrete rather than bricks to reduce the downward pressure.

The GWR board feared they might collapse under the weight of passing trains and so instructed Brunel to keep the wooden framework in place. This he, reluctantly, did but lowered the timbers so that it just appeared to be in place but it had no structural impact on the bridge. It was eventually swept away by floods. The towpath passes under the right-hand arch (facing upstream) and is known as the *Sounding Arch* because of its echo.

Initially the bridge carried two 7 foot gauge railway tracks. However as the popularity of the railways increased it became necessary to introduce standard gauge tracks and the bridge was widened between 1890/2. Each side of the bridge was extended outwards, creating space to carry four standard gauge tracks. This almost doubled the width of the original crossing.

M4 Thames Bridge

This concrete road bridge was built in the 1960s and carries the M4 motorway across the river. There is a pedestrian walkway on either side linking Bray Village and Dorney.

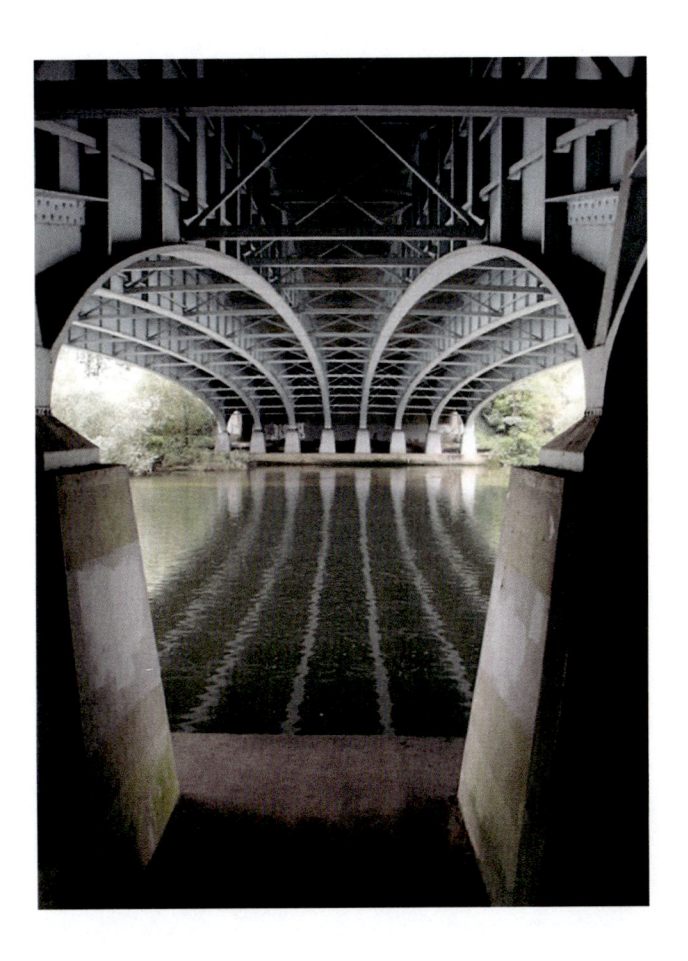

Summerleaze Footbridge

This footbridge was opened in 1996 as a footpath across the river linking the Bray side with the Dorney Olympic rowing course. Originally it was a conveyor belt used in the removal of gravel when building the Eton College (Dorney) course. On completion it was converted to provide access to the rowing lake, taking its name from the constructors.

Thames Crossings 63

Queen Elizabeth Bridge, Windsor

This concrete road bridge, which opened in 1966, carries the Windsor by-pass across the river.

Windsor Railway Bridge

This is a wrought iron, bow & string bridge designed by Isambard King Brunel. It opened in 1849. It is a single span structure comprising three bowstring trusses and designed for the original GWR tracks. It is the world's oldest wrought iron railway bridge still in regular service.

The bridge was built to take two tracks but the track on the upstream side was removed in 1960 and it now carries sewage pipes and a water main. Windsor station is linked to the bridge by a long brick viaduct which, by 1865, had replaced the original wooden trestle structure.

Windsor Town Bridge

Construction started in 1822 and the bridge opened two years later. It has three arches, each comprising of seven cast iron segments, supported in midstream by two granite piles.

There have been many timber bridges on this site. In 1172 *'Osbert de Bray, farmer of Windsor, accounted £4 6s 6d derived from tolls on vessels passing under Windsor Bridge'.* In 1224 and in 1236 reference is made to oak trees felled in Windsor Forest to be used for the construction of the bridge here. In 1443 Eton College is granted free passage over and under the bridge. An Act of Parliament in 1734 set the bridge tolls as follows:

Hearse or coach with a dead body	*6s 8d*
Hackney carriage	*2d*
Score of sheep	*2d*
Head of oxen hogs, cattle or horse load with hampers	*½d*
Every barge going under bridge downstream	*6d*

By 1819 the wooden bridge had so deteriorated that it was decided to build the present bridge in new materials. Built as a road bridge, tolls were levied on crossing traffic. These were scrapped in 1897. In 1970 cracks were discovered in some of the cast iron segments and, despite protests, it was closed to all motorised traffic and remains only open to pedestrians and cyclists.

Black Potts Railway Bridge

This is an iron railway bridge, opened in 1850, which crosses both the Thames and its tributary, the Jubilee River. Originally it had six ornate cast iron ribs, but these corroded and were replaced with wrought iron girders in 1892. It carries the railway line from London Waterloo.

Bridges and Ferries at Datchet

There has been a settlement at Datchet since 990. The first crossing across the Thames was in 1224 when Henry III gave John Passit a *'great oak'* to make a boat. The Crown provided vessels but the rights to operate ferries and collect tolls sat with the Lord of Datchet Manor. Privy Purse records show payment to the Datchet ferry man in 1501, 1522, and 1530.

When William III built a wall on the Windsor bank, complaints were made and in 1699 the Crown bought the ferry rights. This was important for the Crown as it provided a convenient and shorter route for royalty and courtiers travelling from London to Windsor Castle. In 1702 Queen Anne ordered a timber bridge to be made in oak to replace the ferry which, unlike at Maidenhead and Windsor, was toll free. It was a ten arch bridge of wood on stone piers but this collapsed in a flood in 1794 and another ferry reinstated in its place. A third bridge was built on the remaining piers in 1812.

This one also collapsed in 1836 and it was left to the neighbouring counties to fund its replacement. With no agreement they decided each to build their own. Berkshire replaced their half in iron suspended from chains, Buckinghamshire in wood. The two parts did not meet in the middle and so had no structural integrity. As part of the expansion of the grounds of Windsor Castle, and the rerouting of the Datchet and Windsor roads, this bridge was demolished in 1848 and the Victoria and Albert Bridges built to replace it.

Victoria Bridge, Datchet

The 1851 bridge was built of cast iron with stone abutments. The bridge was severely damaged by a group of tanks crossing on exercise in 1944 and eventually closed in 1963 after operating with weight restrictions for many years. A temporary Bailey bridge was erected while the central crossing was replaced by a concrete structure and reopened in 1967.

Albert Bridge, Datchet

The 1851 Albert Bridge was also built in cast iron. It was rebuilt in brick in 1928. The bridge has two large arches that span the river and a stone balustrade.

M25 Bridge, Runnymede

In 1969 a bridge was built to take the A30 over the Thames. A second bridge was then added in 1983 to take the newly constructed M25 around London. Both bridges are single arched bridges made of matching concrete frames, the second taking the same form as the first. In 2005 the motorway bridge was extended to take six lanes.

Staines Bridge

This arched stone bridge, built in white granite, was opened in 1832 with three spans and two piers in the river. It is the fifth bridge on this site. There may have been more than one bridge here in Roman times. In 1228 a grant of two oaks from Windsor Forest was given by the Crown for the repair of Staines Bridge which was *'probably a rough structure of piles with transverse beams'*. In 1262 it consisted of piles of oak driven into the bed of the river and covered in planks. It was put out of use during the Civil War. Ogilby writes in 1699 of a *'wooden bridge maintain'd by a toll on Barges'*.

> *Written in the Westminster Review in 1830*
>
> *About thirty years ago there was, at this place, a wooden bridge, which was condemned, and a stone bridge of three arches was built just below it. This was scarcely finished, when the piers sunk, and the arches cracked; luckily in time to stop the removal of the condemned wooden bridge, which, it was discovered, might be trusted till another new bridge, was completed.*
>
> *It was now taken for granted that the bed of the river could not support piers and an iron bridge of one arch, with comely stone abutments, spanned the Thames with infinite grace. But this again had scarcely been opened, when, under the pressure of a herd of cattle, the Arche stove-in the Middlesex abutment, and again, luckily, in time to stop the removal of the wooden bridge, which, it was again found, would service till the completion of a 3rd new edifice.*
>
> *This was a wooden bridge with an iron railing, of which the piers rooted with a celerity quite edifying; and now, after repeated repairs, this is condemned in its turn, and another stone bridge is in progress, and nearly completed, which will of course last still Doomsday.*

Staines Railway Bridge

This iron railway bridge was completed in 1856. It carries the Waterloo to Reading line. It has two spans and two piers in the river.

M3 Bridge, Chertsey

Built in the 1970s, this is a concrete bridge carrying the M3 across the river in a single span.

Chertsey Bridge

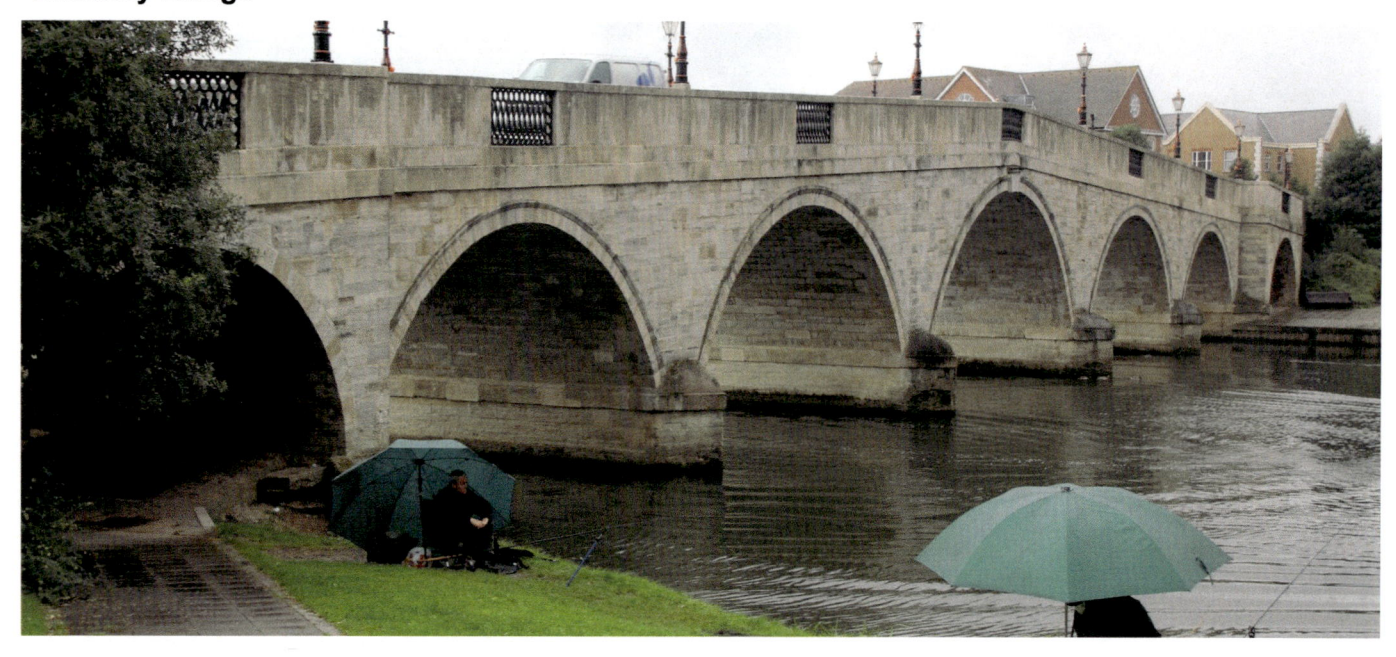

This is a seven arch bridge built of white Purbeck stone and completed in 1784.

In 1299 Sibille, a ferry woman of Chertsey, and her six men were paid 3 shillings for 'wafting' the King and his family across the Thames on his way to Kingston.

Leland writes in 1530 of *'a goodly bridge of timber newly repaired'* but by 1580 it was seriously in need of repair. The bridge slanted upwards from the Middlesex to the Surrey bank. In 1632 it was described *'as the work of a left-handed man'*. The slant was annoying to navigate and it was described as *'very inconvenient and dangerous'*.

Robert Whitworth designed a new bridge in 1780 which was finished in 1784. 184 piles of the old wooden bridge were cut off 6 foot below high water mark and the materials were auctioned off for £120. The bridge was toll free.

The contractor built the number of arches stipulated in the contract, each of which formed a segment of a circle, but they did not fully stretch across the river. So Middlesex and Surrey, who were sharing the costs of the project, had to pay the extra expense for it to reach both sides.

The bridge was partly rebuilt in 1894. Now it has a weight restriction of 18 tonnes .

Shepperton to Weybridge Ferry

The Shepperton to Weybridge Ferry operates from just below Shepperton lock and weir. These were built to regulate the bends and shallows of the river at this point which had been a danger to barge operators over many years. A ferry has been crossing here for over 500 years. It runs on the quarter of the hour and can be summoned by ringing the brass bell provided on each bank. By the 15th Century there were two other ferries close by. The ferry at Walton was replaced by a bridge in 1750 and the ferry to Old Shepperton has now stopped.

Walton Bridge

This modern road bridge is the sixth on the site, constructed of steel in a single span and opened in 2013. It is also on the site of the first ford and a bargee's ferry across the river.

In 1747 Samuel Dicks, a local landowner obtained permission to build the first bridge at Walton. It consisted of *'timbers tangent to a circle of 100 feet diameter'* so that a single timber could be removed and repaired without disruption to the rest of the bridge. It was completed in 1750. It was an elegant structure with a high central arch but it was hard work to drag a large load over it. It stood for 33 years and was dismantled in 1778 after a report stated that decay in the wooden frame made it unsuitable for use. It gained a world-renowned reputation *as 'the most beautiful wooden arch in the world'*. Its matchstick-like intricacies can be seen in Canaletto's painting *A View of Walton Bridge*, 1754 (*oil on canvas, 48.7 x 76.4 cm, DPG600*).

A second, stronger brick and stone bridge replaced it. This one inspired three paintings by Turner. It was opened in 1788 and tolls were charged. A ferry was laid on during its construction. One morning in 1859 the central spans collapsed for no apparent reason and a new bridge was required.

The ferry was again reinstated until completion of the third bridge in 1864. This was an iron girder lattice bridge on stone piers. It was damaged in 1940 during WWII, leading to a permanent weight restriction and restricting use to pedestrians and cyclists.

The fourth bridge was a temporary structure, constructed in 1953 on the downstream side of the third bridge which was demolished in 1985. Another temporary bridge was constructed in 1999 which was used by vehicles to cross, leaving pedestrians and cyclists to cross on the fourth bridge.

by permission of the Trustees of Dulwich Picture Gallery, London

The present, modern bridge replaced the fourth and fifth ones which both had inherent structural weaknesses. Although they remained in use during its construction, both were removed after completion in November 2013.

Hampton Ferry

There has been a ferry operating here since 1514. It enabled fisherman to cross to the seasonally marshy and reed-laden Mulsey Hurst to catch fish. It was incorporated by statute, making the ferry one of the ten oldest established companies in the UK. It operates from March to October and can be summoned by ringing the brass bell on either bank.

Hampton Court Bridge

This bridge has three wide arches, constructed of reinforced concrete and faced with red bricks and white Portland stone. It was opened in 1933.

This has been the site of ferries since Tudor times. The first bridge was made of timber with seven wooden arches and built in the Chinoiserie design of the willow pattern. Privately owned, this bridge was completed in 1753. It was replaced by a sturdier, eleven arched wooden bridge in 1778. By 1840 this had become dilapidated and was described as *'crazy, hog-backed, inconvenient and obstructive to navigation'*.

It was replaced by a third bridge, which opened in 1866. This was constructed of wrought iron lattice girders, resting on four cast iron columns. Although criticised as *'one of the ugliest bridges in England, and a flagrant eyesore and disfigurement both to the river and to Hampton Court',* it proved very lucrative and earned its owner, Thomas Allen, over £3,000 annually in tolls. He sold it in 1876 for £48,048 to the Corporation of London. While the present bridge was being built just downstream of it, the third bridge, remained open to traffic and was demolished on the completion of its successor.

Kingston Bridge

A new Kingston Bridge opened in 1828. It was built of Portland stone and consisted of five elliptical arches. It became toll free in 1870. Double tramlines crossed the bridge in 1906, making it very narrow and so in 1914 it was widened between the parapets. It was widened again in 2001 when the existing bridge was strengthened and a new one, in mirror image, built alongside.

This is one of the oldest sites for bridges on the river. The Charter Quay archaeological dig revealed that the island of Kingston was planned as a new town. In 1170 four timber bridges were built to cross the Thames here but in 1224 only one remained. By 1318 this was in a dangerous condition. In 1449 *'a grant of portage was granted to the bailiffs and good men of Kingston'* for repair of the bridge and the building of a causeway.

It was damaged during the Wars of the Roses and again, in 1554, during Wyatt's rebellion. On a post in the middle of this bridge is this inscription in brass: *'1567 Robert Hamon, Gentleman, Bayliffe of Kingstone, heretofore that then made this Bryge toolfre for evermore'*. Hamon endowed the bridge with £40 annually to cover the costs of maintaining the structure.

In 1710 the bridge was described: *'The great Wooden Bridge hath 20 interstices, two in the middle wide enough for barges...it had 22 pierres of Wood and had in the middle two fair Seates for Passengers to avoid Carts and to sit and enjoy the delightfull Prospect'*.

By the early 19th Century the bridge's state of repair was problematic. It had become increasingly dilapidated and its narrowness made passage difficult both for river and road traffic. In 1802 *'a new arch is most wanting; the present navigation arch is very dangerous, several barges having been sunk across the bridge'*. When a severe frost caused part of the bridge to collapse in 1814, it was obvious that a new bridge was required and building eventually began on the present bridge in 1825.

Kingston Railway Bridge

Kingston Railway Bridge is closest in the photograph. It is downstream from Kingston Bridge. The railway bridge was constructed in steel in 1863 and replaced a cast iron bridge. It has five arches with two piers in the river.

The Tidal Thames

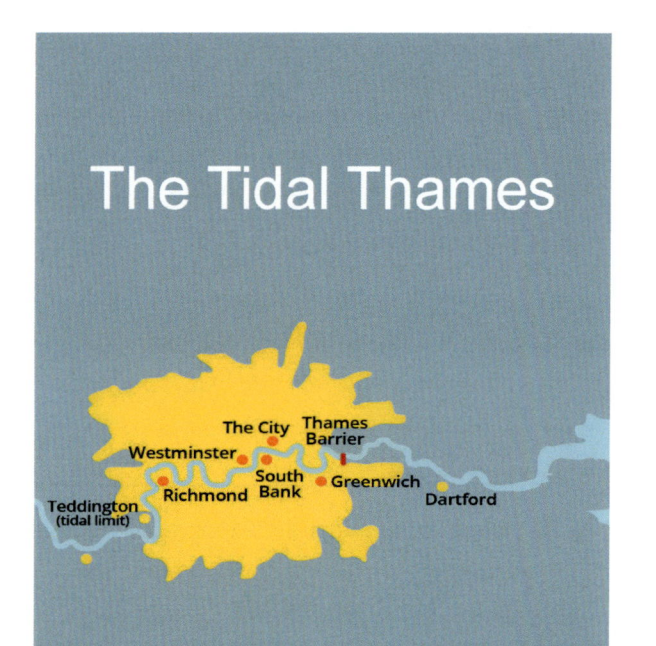

Teddington to Tilbury

This is the Thames's tidal section where, depending on the time of year, the river can rise and fall twice a day, by as much as 7m. After Teddington the river wriggles northward and then eastwards through central London. It widens and seems to solidify into a steady, grey-brown flow as it relentlessly moves through the capital. Its surface is broken by the swirls and curls of the currents of water moving downstream and then the meeting up, in a light frenzy, with the regular push of salt water that heads upstream on each tide. Apartment blocks in all sorts of shapes and sizes and textures, glass-fronted office blocks, converted docks, pubs or restaurants with Dickensian names, shopping centres, industrial complexes, traffic depots, abandoned docks and quays and wharves rub shoulders with each other along both banks. Finally, the Thames Barrier is passed - a line of sentries guarding the capital against any wet invader. The river, sighing in exhausted relief, then flops out under the magnificently elegant Queen Elizabeth II Bridge into the North Sea, bidding farewell to our shores and the landscape and the history that it has helped to carve and form.

Crossing	Date
Teddington Lock Footbridges	1889
Hammerton's Ferry	1909
Richmond Road & Railway Bridges	1777 & 1848
Twickenham Bridge	1933
Richmond Lock Footbridges	1894
Kew Bridge	1903
Kew Railway Bridge	1869
Chiswick Bridge	1933
Barnes Railway & Pedestrian Bridge	1895
Hammersmith Bridge	1887
Putney Bridge	1886
Fulham Railway & Pedestrian Bridge	1889
Wandsworth Bridge	1940
Battersea Railway & Road Bridges	1863 & 1890
Albert Bridge	1873
Chelsea Bridge	1937
Grosvenor Railway Bridge	1860
Vauxhall Bridge	1904
Lambeth Bridge	1930
Westminster Bridge	1862
Hungerford & Golden Jubilee Bridges	1845 & 2002
Waterloo Bridge	1945
Blackfriars Bridge	1869
Blackfriars Railway Bridge	1886
Millenium Footbridge	2000
Southwark Bridge	1921
Cannon Street Railway Bridge	1866
London Bridge	1973
Tower Bridge	1894
Rotherhithe Tunnel	1908
Canary Wharf to Rotherhithe Ferry	
Greenwich Foot Tunnel	1902
Blackwall Tunnels	1897
Emirates Air Line	2012
Woolwich Free Ferry	1889
Woolwich Foot Tunnel	1912
The Dartford Crossing	1963
Gravesend to Tilbury Ferry	<1571

Teddington Lock Footbridges

Teddington Lock opened in 1811. The crossing here is formed by two separate bridges funded by local residents and businesses and built between 1887/9. The eastern bridge is an iron girder bridge crossing the lock cut.

The western bridge is a suspension bridge that crosses the weir stream. The weir consists of 34 radial gates, 37 sluice gates and its crescent shape has an overall length of 222 metres.

Hammerton's Ferry

Ferries have crossed the river to the east of here at Richmond since 1459 and to the west at Eel Pie Island since 1652. There was little demand for a ferry crossing at this spot until 1909 when local resident, Walter Hammerton, started a regular ferry service. He used a twelve passenger, clipper-built skiff, charging 1d per trip. The ferry still runs every weekend and weekdays between February and October, operating from a floating boathouse on the north bank to a jetty on the south. It has the right of way over any rowing craft and so races at the Twickenham regatta have to be carefully timed.

Thames Crossings 73

Richmond Bridge

This is a stone arched bridge built between 1774 and 1777 as a replacement for a ferry crossing which had existed here since Norman times.

The earliest known crossing, a ferry, dates from 1439. This was owned by the crown A small skiff was operated to carry passengers with a larger boat used for horses and small carts. However, due to a steep hill down to the river, carriages and heavily laden carts could not use either of the ferries and had to detour via Kingston Bridge.

In the 18th century Richmond and Twickenham became fashionable places to live and the ferry was unable to meet the demands of the area. Local resident William Windham, who leased the ferry and land at the time, sought Parliamentary approval to build a wooden bridge to replace the ferry, funded by tolls. The Richmond Bridge Act was passed in 1772 which stipulated that only tolls could be used to finance the bridge, specified what these were to be and gave compensation to the owner of the ferry. It even imposed severe penalties for *'wilful or malicious damage'* to the structure including the *'transportation to one of his Majesty's Colonies in America for the space of 7 years'*. It became a commercial success taking £1,300 in tolls in 1810.

By the early 20th century the bridge was inadequate for the increasing traffic and in 1931 proposals were made to widen it. Due to local objections it was decided to build a new bridge downstream and Twickenham Bridge was opened in 1933. Richmond was still unable to handle the traffic and so in 1934 it was decided to widened the bridge. Each stone on the upstream side was removed and numbered, the bridge widened by 11 feet, the stones were then reassembled and the bridge reopened to traffic in 1940. The road bed at the centre was lowered slightly and the access ramps were raised, thus reducing the hump-backed appearance of the bridge. It is currently the oldest surviving bridge on the Thames in London and has been described as a *'simple and elegant structure'*.

Richmond Railway Bridge

Originally built in 1848 with three 100 foot, cast iron girders the bridge was supported on stone-faced arches, two being river piers and the other on land. The bridge was rebuilt in 1902, reusing the existing piers and abutments and the bridge girders and decking were replaced in 1924.

Twickenham Bridge

Twickenham Bridge opened in 1933 with three reinforced concrete arches, supported on concrete piers. The UK's first speed camera was installed here in 1992. This was the original site of the Twickenham Ferry.

Thames Crossings 75

Richmond Lock Bridges

In 1832 the old London Bridge was removed after the opening of the new bridge a year earlier. As a result water levels at Teddington were lowered by as much as 2½ feet (about a metre) and the Thames at Twickenham and Richmond was sometimes little more than a stream running between mud banks.

In 1890 permission was granted to build a barge lock downstream of Richmond Bridge, on the Surrey bank, with a roller slipway for small craft on the Middlesex bank, connected by a weir.

A superstructure was constructed in 1894 to operate the sluice gates mechanism. This maintained the water level upstream. Originally this was hand cranked but now it is raised by electric power.

The gantry took the form of 2 parallel footbridges, each 100 metres long. On payment of a toll pedestrians could cross the river using these walkways. In 1938 the 1d payment was abolished. A major refurbishment took place in the 1990s. The lock is owned and run by the Port of London Authority.

Kew Bridge

The present bridge, immediately adjacent to the Royal Botanic Gardens on the Kew side, was built by Middlesex and Surrey County Councils and opened in 1903. It is constructed of granite from Cornwall with three elliptical arches which are decorated with the carvings of the ornamental shields of the two counties.

The first bridge at Kew was built in 1759 when Robert Tunstall of Brentford, who owned the ferry here, built two stone arches on each bank with seven timber arches in between. This bridge was costly to maintain and only lasted thirty years. Tolls were charged to cross it, ranging from 1d for pedestrians and 1/6d for a coach & 4 horses.

Tunstall's son, Robert, obtained permission to replace it with a second bridge of stone alongside the first, which remained in place during construction. The new bridge opened in 1789. Tolls were set at a 1/2d per pedestrian and 6d for each horse. But the approach was too narrow and steep on the Brentford side and the bridge could not cope with the weight of traffic.

It was decided to replace it. Construction on the present bridge started in 1899 after a temporary, wooden bridge had been built and the second bridge demolished.

Kew Railway Bridge

Kew Railway Bridge, also known as the Strand-on-the-Green Bridge, was opened in 1869. It consists of five wrought iron lattice girders, each with a 35 metre span, on cast iron columns with ornate capitals. It is now owned by Network Rail.

Chiswick Bridge

Along with the bridge at Twickenham, this bridge was built here at Chiswick in 1933. It is a concrete structure, faced with Portland stone on concrete foundations. It has five spans, with the smaller two at either end over the towpaths. It has two piers in the water.

The ferry, which had been operating here since at least the 17th Century, linked Chiswick and Mortlake, both sparsely populated at the time. But after WWI the population in the suburbs grew, as did car ownership, and the congestion in the narrow local streets became chronic. The ferry was no longer able to meet demand so the present bridge was built. The ferry closed on completion of the bridge.

The University Boat Race is, surprisingly, rowed upstream with the incoming tide and the finish is marked, just below Chiswick Bridge, by the University Stone on the south bank and the University Post on the north bank.

Barnes Railway & Pedestrian Bridge

This two track railway bridge was completed in 1895, consisting of three spans made of wrought iron girders. Pedestrians can also use the bridge to cross the river. A cast iron bridge was first built here in 1849 as part of a loop around Richmond for passenger and freight traffic. It remains unused alongside the present bridge. During its construction in 1847/8 the Boat Race was cancelled for safety reasons.

Hammersmith Bridge

This suspension bridge was built on the same pier foundations as a previous one on this site. It opened in 1887. The superstructure uses eight wrought iron chains slung between stone suspension towers. Vertical rods are suspended from them to support cross girders, deck timbers and tarmac. It has never really coped with the weight and volume of road traffic, requiring frequent refurbishment and repairs. At each end there is a motif made up of seven coats of arms – the Royal Arms of the UK, the City of London, Kent, Guildford, the City of Westminster, Colchester and Middlesex.

The first bridge was built here in 1825 as a toll bridge. By the 1870s it was no longer strong enough to support the weight of traffic wanting to cross over the river. The problem was exacerbated each year when 11/12000 people crowded onto the bridge and its chains to watch the boat race:

'*1868 – Hammersmith Bridge is impassable and almost invisible, every available inch of standing or hanging room, from the pavement to the chains, close covered with expectant sight seers till the roadway sinks under the pressure, eighteen inches below its orthodox level'.*

A temporary bridge was erected in 1884 while work on the present bridge took place.

In 2000, following a bomb attack, the bridge was repainted in its original colour.

Thames Crossings 79

Putney Bridge

1886 saw the completion of this new five span bridge, built of stone and Cornish granite, slightly upstream from the first bridge that was built here in 1729 on the site of a ferry. The previous bridge was a timber toll bridge with 26 openings. People were reluctant to pay the tolls, after all London Bridge was free, and so two toll collectors were stationed at each end and given staves to persuade the public to pay. Bells were hung from the tops of the toll towers to summon help from colleagues when required. This old bridge was bought by the Metropolitan Board of Works in 1879 and they replaced it with the present bridge. It is the only bridge in UK to have a church at both ends – St Mary's, Putney and All Saints Church, Fulham. It is also the site of the Putney Aqueduct that brought fresh water from above Teddington, built in 1856. The University Boat Race starts upstream from Putney Bridge.

Fulham Railway & Pedestrian Bridge

The bridge was built in 1889 and consists of five turquoise wrought iron, lattice girders, supported on pairs of cast iron cylinders. When it was first built, Fulham was mostly countryside. Day trippers would cross the river on the downstream walkway to enjoy the fresh air or one of the many boat trips that were available on the far bank.

Wandsworth Bridge

The present steel cantilever bridge was opened in 1940.

The first structure was built here in 1873. It had been a wrought iron toll bridge with a timber roadway. It was commercially unsuccessful because an expected railway terminus on the north bank failed to materialise. There were also difficulties with access to the bridge due to drainage problems on the south bank. In 1880 it was taken into public ownership and the tolls were abolished. It was demolished in 1937 being too narrow and too weak to carry buses. It was replaced by the present bridge.

Battersea Railway Bridge

Originally called the Cremorne Bridge, after the pleasure grounds in Chelsea, this bridge was opened in 1863. It carries two sets of railway lines on four lattice girder arches set on four stone piers.

Battersea Bridge

The present bridge is only twelve metres wide and is the capital's narrowest road bridge across the Thames. It opened in 1890. It consists of five arches of cast iron girders on granite piers. Trams used Battersea Bridge from the start. Initially they were horse-drawn and then, in 1911, the tram network was electrified.

Chelsea has existed as a settlement since Anglo-Saxon times. The Thames bends sharply here and becomes slow moving, thus making it easy to ford. The area is mentioned in the Domesday Book as having asparagus and lavender industries. A ferry has existed here since at least 1550 when a ferryman gave evidence at the Old Bailey following an incident on his ferry. Some of his passengers were sentenced to death following a robbery.

By 1766 the ferry was old and dangerous and John Earl Spencer formed the Battersea Bridge Company to build a stone toll bridge here. Not enough people invested in the scheme and so only a timber bridge was built which opened to pedestrians in 1771 and vehicle traffic a year later. It was poorly designed with 19 narrow arches and boats often collided with it. To reduce the danger to shipping, two piers were removed and the sections above were reinforced with iron girders. It was never a commercial success despite the tolls charged. It required constant repair and whenever it was closed, the owners had to lay on a ferry. In 1790 it was the first bridge over the river to be lit.

In 1844 a woman was murdered on the bridge in full view of the toll collectors who did not intervene as both parties had paid their money.

In 1879 The Metropolitan Board of Works bought Battersea Bridge in a job lot with Albert Bridge and tolls were abolished on both. By 1883 it was in such poor condition that access was restricted to pedestrians. It was demolished in 1885 and work on the new bridge started two years later. This present bridge still presents a hazard to navigation in modern times, with collisions taking place on numerous occasions.

Albert Bridge

Albert Bridge started life in 1873 as a cable-stayed bridge. To make it structurally stronger elements of a suspension bridge were added between 1884 and 1887. Then in 1973 two concrete piers were added which turned the central span into a beam bridge.

It was built as a toll bridge but this was commercially unsuccessful and it was taken into public ownership six years after opening. However, the toll booths remain and are the only examples of such buildings in London. The bridge is nicknamed the 'Trembling Lady' because when large numbers of people cross it together it vibrates. There are signs at each end instructing marching troops to 'break step' when crossing.

Structurally weak, it was always ill-equipped to deal with modern traffic but it is still one of two London bridges never to have been replaced.

Chelsea Bridge

The first self-anchored suspension bridge in the UK, Chelsea Bridge, opened in 1937.

The first bridge here was a suspension bridge which opened in 1857 as part of the redevelopment of the marshlands on the south bank of the Thames. It linked the densely populated north bank to the newly developed Battersea Park. It was built and operated by the government and tolls were charged to try to recoup the costs. This was unpopular, so Sundays became toll-free.

The bridge struggled as a commercial enterprise partly because of competition from the newly built Albert Bridge nearby. It was acquired by the Metropolitan Board of Works in 1877 and tolls were abolished completely two years later.

Originally called Victoria Bridge it was renamed Chelsea Bridge to avoid any association between the royal family and this narrow, unsound crossing. It was eventually demolished to be replaced by the present structure.

Grosvenor Railway Bridge

Built in 1860, this was the first railway bridge to cross the Thames in central London. It was widened a number of times but eventually, between 1963 and 1967, it was rebuilt and strengthened. It consists of parallel bridges carrying ten tracks into Victoria train station.

Vauxhall Bridge

Construction of this new bridge started here in 1904 and it opened two years later. Granite piers support a steel superstructure. Alfred Drury and Frederick Pomeroy were then appointed to improve its functional appearance by carving huge statues, each weighing several tons. Drury, on the upstream piers, depicts science, fine arts, local government and education. Pomeroy's downstream piers depict agriculture, architecture, engineering and pottery.

The remains of the oldest prehistoric bridge in Britain have been found just upstream from Vauxhall, taking the form of two lines of oak posts dating to between 1750BC and 1285BC (the middle Bronze Age). It is thought that the bridge would have been made of planks resting on the lines of posts. The posts were about 5 metres apart and angled inwards forming a cradle. At the time the river would have consisted of a number of shallow channels spreading over the marshy land.

The first 'proper' bridge was built here, on the site of Huntley Ferry, opening in 1816. It was the first iron bridge across the Thames and consisted of nine cast iron arches on stone piers. Originally it was called Robert Bridge and renamed Vauxhall Bridge shortly afterwards. The owners of Battersea Bridge were paid compensation for the loss of custom and the drop in revenue. Tolls were set on a sliding scale from 1d for pedestrians to 2s 6d for vehicles drawn by six horses. There were exceptions for mail coaches, soldiers on duty, and Parliamentary candidates at election time.

Revenues were not as high as expected as the bridge was mainly used by the workers living in the tenements around the Doulton stoneware factory on the south bank, rather than any wealthy residents who were not drawn to the area. However, usage did increase with the building, in 1838, of the terminus of the London and South West Railway. When that closed, the bridge was used to access Vauxhall Gardens Pleasure Park from where balloon flights took place.

As with other London bridges, Vauxhall Bridge was taken over by the Metropolitan Board of Works who abolished tolls in 1879. In 1898 a temporary wooden bridge was constructed, the old bridge was demolished and the new one constructed at the same spot. The contractor paid £50 for the timber and scrap metal from the temporary structure when it was dismantled. Initially horse-drawn trams used the bridge but by 1911 London County Council had electrified the tram network which included Vauxhall Bridge. It was the first road in London to have bus lanes.

Lambeth Bridge

Lambeth bridge opened in 1932. It has five spans and is of steel construction with granite facings painted red. This contrasts with the next bridge downstream at Westminster which is painted green. Between them, they match the colour of the benches in the Houses of Parliament. At either end of the bridge there is a pair of obelisks topped by stone pinecones; or are they pineapples, symbols of friendship and hospitality, or a tribute to local resident, **John Tradescant**, said to have grown the first pineapple in the UK?

The first mention of a horse-drawn ferry (Horseferry) operating from here was made in 1367. It linked Lambeth Palace with the Palace of Westminster. The clerks of Chancery paid £16 to the keepers of the barge for transporting the Archbishop of Canterbury across the Thames to his house at Lambeth. In 1513 Humphrey Trevilyen was granted the right to operate the ferry on payment of 16d per annum. An overloaded boat sank in 1656 with servants and horses being thrown into the water, including Lord Cromwell's coach. In 1750, when Westminster Bridge opened, the archbishop surrendered the rights to the ferry and was compensated for ceasing its operation.

The first bridge, a suspension bridge, opened in 1869. It was considered unsafe from the start with awkward, steep approaches which deterred horse-drawn vehicles. It was used almost solely as a pedestrian crossing. It ceased to be a toll bridge in 1879. By then it had become severely corroded and by 1910 it was closed to vehicles. After long delays caused by floods and the redevelopment of Chelsea Embankment, work started on the present bridge in 1928.

Westminster Bridge

The present wrought iron, seven arched bridge opened in 1862 and is the oldest road bridge across the Thames in central London. It is painted green. This contrasts with Lambeth Bridge which is painted red. Between them, they match the colours of the benches in the Houses of Parliament.

A bridge at Westminster was first proposed in 1664, but opposed by the Corporation of London and the watermen who operated ferries across the river at this point. Despite further opposition in 1722, the scheme received parliamentary approval in 1736, with the watermen getting £25,000 in compensation (£2 million in modern day terms). The stone bridge was built between 1739 and 1750. Construction of this, and other London bridges at the time, was facilitated by a new invention. Powered by horses winding up a heavy weight, the pile driver was designed to ram each of its 14 piers hard into the river bed.

By the mid 19th Century the bridge was subsiding badly and it had become expensive to maintain, so the decision was taken to replace it.

Hungerford & Golden Jubilee Bridges

Also known as Charing Cross Bridge, it opened in 1845 as a suspension footbridge designed by Isambard Kingdom Brunel. Then South East Railways bought it, and replaced it with nine spans of wrought iron lattice girders which opened ten years later (the chains were later reused in the Clifton Suspension Bridge). Walkways were added on each side. The upstream walkway was later removed when the railway was widened in 1886 to increase the number of tracks from four to eight.

The remaining footbridge was narrow, dilapidated and dangerous, so, in the mid 1990s, a competition was held to design a new walkway using the existing brick piers. The work was completed in 2002.

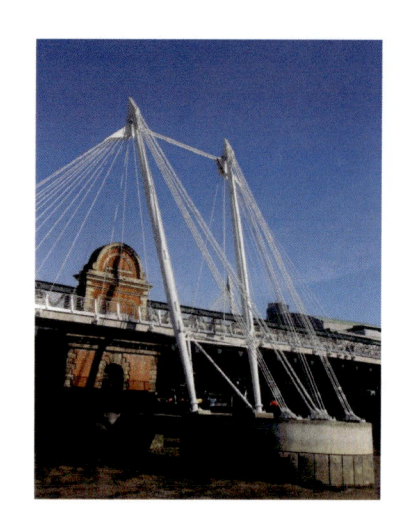

Waterloo Bridge

Partially opened in 1942, and completed in 1945, it was the only bridge to be damaged by German bombers in WWII. Most of the workers were women so it is sometimes referred to as the Ladies Bridge. It is constructed with concrete beams clad with Portland stone. Within each pier a couple of jacks can level the structure in the event of subsidence in the river bed.

This was a constant problem with the first bridge, which opened in 1817 to commemorate the Battle of Waterloo. The bridge was built of granite with nine arches. From 1884 serious problems were found with the brick piers and renovations had to be made. Eventually, due to this settlement, it was decided to demolish the bridge and replace it with this new structure.

Blackfriars Bridge

The present bridge, consisting of five wrought iron arches, was designed by Joseph Cubitt, and opened by Queen Victoria in 1869. He also designed the adjacent railway bridge which has since been demolished. The spans and piers of both bridges had to align to aid navigation. The ends of the bridge are shaped like a pulpit in reference to the Franciscan Black Friars who had a monastery on the north bank.

On the piers of the bridge are stone carvings of water birds by sculptor John Birnie Philip. On the piers facing east, the downstream side, the side closest to the Thames Estuary and the North Sea, the carvings show marine life and seabirds. Those facing west, the upstream side, show freshwater birds. This reflects the fact that Blackfriars is the tidal turning point of the river. On the north side of the bridge is a statue of Queen Victoria.

The first fixed crossing at Blackfriars was a long toll bridge designed in an Italianate style by Robert Mylne and constructed with nine semi-elliptical arches of Portland stone. It took nine years to build, opening to the public in 1769. It was the third bridge across the Thames in the then built-up area of London. The workmanship was faulty and between 1833 and 1840 repeated extensive repairs were necessary. Eventually it was decided to build the new bridge on the same site.

Blackfriars Railway Bridge

The first bridge here opened in 1864. The use of the bridge gradually declined as Waterloo became the main station. When it also became too weak to carry modern trains it was removed leaving a series of columns across the river. The second bridge was built downstream. Originally called St Paul's Railway Bridge, it opened in 1886.

As part of the Thameslink Programme, the platforms of the old Blackfriars station were extended along the bridge and across the river, partially supported on the 1864 bridge piers. The roof is covered with solar panels and it is the largest of only three solar bridges in the world.

Millennium Footbridge

Initially, this steel suspension walkway opened in 2000. On the first day, the large number of pedestrians using the bridge caused a severe swaying motion. The 'Wobbly Bridge' was immediately closed to remedy the problem and did not reopen until 2002. It is owned and maintained by Bridge House Estates.

Southwark Bridge

It has five steel arches which are designed so the four stone piers line up with those at Blackfriars and London Bridges to help passing river traffic. It opened in 1921 replacing a previous cast iron bridge, Queen Street Bridge, a toll bridge which went bankrupt because neighbouring bridges could be used for free. Bridge House Estates bought the bridge in 1864 and made it toll free. They own and maintain the present bridge.

Cannon Street Railway Bridge

This opened in 1866 and was renovated between 1979 and 1982. It carries the railway over the Thames on five spans, standing on cast iron Doric pillars.

London Bridge

The present bridge took five years to build and was opened in 1973. It is a box girder bridge with three spans, built of concrete and steel.

From early days the river could be easily crossed here due to the height of the embankments on either side, by ford at low tide and by ferry at high tide. The first London bridge was built here by the Romans. It was a pontoon which followed the line of Watling Street. This was replaced by a permanent timber piled bridge in 55AD but it fell into disrepair when the Romans left Britain.

King Canute refers to a Saxon bridge being here in 1016, which he had to cut through to bring his ships up the Thames. In 1066 King William I rebuilt the bridge. There were two more rebuilds, again in timber- in 1091 following a tornado, and in 1163, after it was destroyed by fire.

Henry II commissioned a new stone bridge in 1176 with a chapel in the middle, dedicated to Thomas Becket. This was the starting point for his pilgrimage to Canterbury following the murder of the archbishop. He raised the funds to build the bridge with taxes on sheepskins and wool.

It took 33 years to build and was finished in 1209 in the reign of King John. It was 8 metres wide, supported by 19 irregularly spaced arches with a drawbridge in the middle to allow the passage of tall ships.

By 1358, 138 shops crowded along the bridge along with several multi-seated latrines that overhung the parapet over the river. Not only were these buildings a fire hazard but they also increased the load on its arches which frequently had to be rebuilt.

'View of Old London Bridge from the West', Claude de Jongh, 1650 © **Victoria and Albert Museum, London**

By Tudor times there were over two hundred buildings on the bridge, some seven stories high, some overhanging the river by several feet and some almost touching in the middle thus creating a dark tunnel. The roadway was twelve feet wide, six feet in each direction, and was very congested. Crossing the bridge could take as long as an hour and many preferred to use the ferries alongside. The narrow arches and the wide pier bases of the bridge itself restricted the ebb and flow of the tide and the waters upstream were susceptible to freezing.

To make things worse, in the 15th century water mills were built on piers on each bank, two to the north of the bridge to power water pumps and two to the south to power grain mills. This caused a difference in water levels as great as two metres and produced ferocious rapids between the piers. *'The bridge was for wise men to pass over and for fools to pass under'.*

Over the southern gatehouse heads of traitors, dipped in tar to preserve them, were impaled on spikes. Over the years these have included William Wallace, Jack Cade, Thomas More and Thomas Cromwell. In 1598 there were as many as thirty displayed over the gates.

By 1722 congestion was so serious that the Lord Mayor decreed that *'all carts, coaches and other carriages coming out of Southwark into this city do keep all along the west side of said bridge; and all carts and coaches going out of the city do keep along the east side'.* Is this the origin of the Brits driving on the left?

Following an Act of Parliament, between 1758 and 1762 all the houses and shops on the bridge were demolished and the two central arches were replaced by a single central span to improve navigation.

By the end of the 18th century, the bridge, by then over 600 years old, was narrow and decrepit and blocked river traffic and the time had come for it to be replaced. John Rennie won the competition to design a new bridge and work started in 1824 with the medieval bridge being used until it was demolished after the new bridge, its five arches built of granite, was opened in 1831.

In 1896 the bridge was the busiest point in London, and one of its most congested, 8,000 pedestrians and 900 vehicles crossed every hour. But, and a big but, it was sinking at the rate of one inch every eight years and by 1924 the east side was 3 to 4 inches below the west side. It needed replacing.

In 1967 the City of London Council placed the bridge on the market and it was bought by the oil tycoon, Robert McCulloch. Each piece was numbered, shipped to California via the Panama Canal and re-assembled in Arizona. Work then started on the present bridge.

Tower Bridge

Tower Bridge is the first to be built on the tidal section of the Thames. A conventional bridge at this point would prevent tall-masted ships from reaching the Pool of London, a section of the river south of the City of London that was lined with nearly continuous walls of wharves and quays running for miles along both banks. Before its construction, the only way to cross the Thames along this stretch was to use the many ferries run by the watermen or to use the tunnels that were dug, at great expense, beneath the river.

The bridge is a combined bascule and suspension structure, based on the medieval drawbridge, which opened in 1894. The two bridge towers house operating machinery, originally powered by a steam engine, for raising the bascules. The upper level horizontal walkways withstand the tension forces of the suspension structure on the landward side of each of the towers.

The walkways were closed in 1910 as they had a reputation for the presence of prostitutes and pickpockets. Underneath the bridge, the Tower Subway was opened in 1870. This housed one of the world's first underground railways but it closed three months after opening. It reopened as a tolled, pedestrian foot tunnel, but once a toll-free Tower Bridge was in operation there was no demand for the crossing and the tunnel was closed in 1898. The bridge was modernised in 1982 with covered walkways and an exhibition centre. With 24 hours notice, it can be opened for shipping to pass through. This happens about 1,000 times a year.

Rotherhithe Tunnel

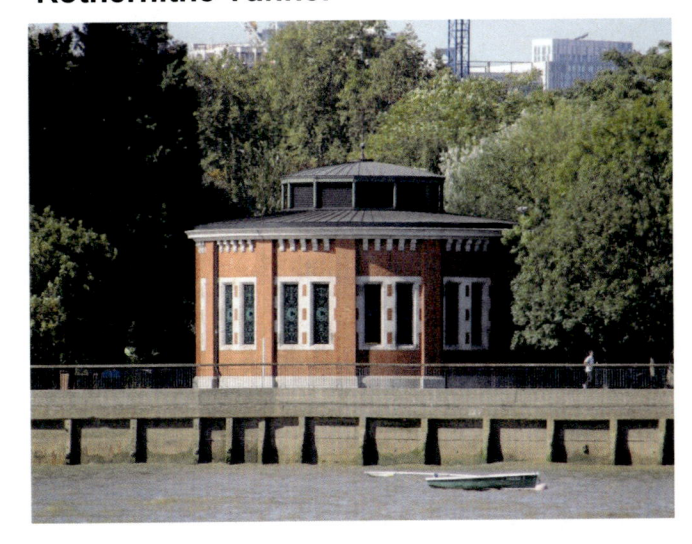

On the surface, the only evidence of this underground road crossing, which opened in 1908, are the two ventilator shafts on either bank. Each contains a spiral staircase for pedestrian access but both are now closed to the public. Cars, bicycles and pedestrians enter the tunnel by the brick-lined cutting at each end of the tunnel. It was designed to take foot and horse-drawn traffic between the docks on either side of the river and has a kink in the middle to prevent horses from bolting.

Close by is the Thames Tunnel which was the first tunnel to be built under a navigable river and built between 1825 and 1843 using shield technology. It was designed for, but never used by, horse-drawn carriages and is now used by London Overground.

Canary Wharf to Rotherhithe Ferry

This passenger ferry continues the long tradition of cross river ferries operated by ferrymen. It operates between Canary Wharf Pier and the Nelson Dock Pier at the Hilton Hotel, running every 10 minutes at peak times.

Greenwich Foot Tunnel

The Greenwich Foot Tunnel crosses beneath the river, linking Greenwich with the Isle of Dogs. It opened in 1902, replacing an expensive and unreliable ferry service, which enabled workers living on the south bank to cross to their workplaces in the docks and shipyards over the river.

The cast iron tunnel links Greenwich town centre, next door to the restored clipper Cutty Sark, to Docklands and Canary Wharf. The northern entrance to the tunnel is in Island Gardens which looks across the river to the former Greenwich Hospital, the Queen's House and the Royal Greenwich Observatory.

The entrance shafts at each bank lie beneath glass domes. Within each building a spiral stairway leads down to the sloping, tile-lined tunnel. Cyclists use lifts although they then have to walk their bicycles through the tunnel.

Blackwall Tunnels

These are two tunnels taking road traffic under the river. A single bore tunnel was opened in 1897 to improve trade and commerce in the East End of London. This one has several sharp bends in it to prevent horses from bolting. By the 1930s the capacity was inadequate and a second bore was opened in 1967 to take southbound traffic. The ventilator towers to the new tunnel can be seen at the O2 Arena. Horse-drawn traffic was banned in 1947 and pedestrians and cyclists in 1969.

Emirates Air Line

This is a cable car crossing, sponsored by the Emirates Airline, which opened in 2012. A trip across normally takes 10 minutes although the speed is increased during rush hour to reduce journey time to 5 minutes. There are 36 passenger gondolas, each with a capacity of 10 passengers. Bicycles can also be carried.

The Woolwich Free Ferry

This is a free vehicle ferry linking the North and South Circular roads around London. Three ferries, built in 1963 are in use on the Roll On/Roll Off service. They take ten minutes to cross between the two terminals which were opened in 1966. There has been a ferry here since the 14th century. This was sold in 1320 for 100 silver marks. Originally paddle steamers were used when the free service started in 1889.

Woolwich Foot Tunnel

Just a few metres downstream from the ferry terminal is the pedestrian tunnel, which opened in 1912. This is used by pedestrians to cross if the ferry is, for any reason, not working. Its entrance shafts are hidden in amongst a shopping centre on one side and an apartment block on the other.

The Dartford Crossing

Two bored tunnels and a bridge take the M25 across the estuary. The first tunnel was started in the 1930s but work was interrupted by the war. The tunnel was eventually opened in 1963, taking a single line of traffic in each direction, with a toll set at 2s/6d. Very quickly, this proved to be inadequate and a second tunnel was dug, opening in 1980.

The M25 orbital motorway around London was completed in 1986 and it connected to either end of these tunnels. Work then started on the Queen Elizabeth II Bridge. This cable-stayed bridge was opened in 1991. Southbound traffic used the bridge's four lanes with north bound traffic using the four lanes of the two tunnels. Tolls have always been applied, from 2014 as a electronic payment scheme.

Gravesend to Tilbury Ferry

This is the last public crossing point before the Thames reaches the sea. A sketch map of 1571 shows evidence of two jetties on each marshy bank and it is suggested that a ferry was used to transport sheep and wool across the estuary.

The rights to the ferry were purchased by Gravesend Town Council in 1694 and in the same year, the governor of Tilbury Fort obtained rights for a ferry in the opposite direction. Originally sailing and rowing boats were used to make the crossing but these were replaced by a steam ferry service in 1855.

In 1862 the London, Tilbury and Southend Railway bought the rights from the two companies and successfully operated the service until 1984. Car ferries were introduced in 1927 but were discontinued in 1964 with the opening of the first Dartford Tunnel. The ferry is now operated by the Lower Thames and Medway Passenger Boat Company and boats leave every 30 minutes, 6am to 7pm, Monday to Saturday.

Managing the River

Oxford-Burcot Commission 1605

In the 17th century Burcot was an important transhipment point on the Thames. The river between Oxford and Burcot had, at that time, become almost unnavigable so that goods for Oxford had to be unloaded at Burcot and taken on by road. This led in 1605 to the formation of the Oxford-Burcot Commission to improve navigation. This body built locks at Iffley and Sandford in 1633 and also at Swift Ditch near Abingdon.

Thames Navigation Commissioners 1751

This organisation was established in 1751 and built eight locks between Shiplake and Boulters from 1770 to 1773. They did not interfere with the jurisdiction of the City of London who only handed over their inventory in 1857. The completion of the Thames and Severn Canal to Letchlade in 1789 led to the commissioners building more locks upstream from Shiplake.

Thames Conservancy 1866

In 1866, the Thames Conservancy took over management of the river from Cricklade to Yantlet Creek, a distance of 177 miles (285 km). It was said that the Thames Commissioners were too numerous, the locks and weirs were in a bad condition and income was insufficient to pay for maintenance. All locks canals and other works of the commissioners were transferred to the Conservancy, as was responsibility for all weirs, most of which belonged to the 28 water-mills still operating between Oxford and Staines.

Port of London Authority 1908

Responsibility for the river below Teddington Lock, including Richmond Lock, fell to the Port of London Authority in 1908.

Thames Water Authority 1974

In 1974 Thames Conservancy became Thames Water Authority.

National Rivers Authority 1990

With the privatisation of the water supply in 1990, the river management function passed to the National Rivers Authority.

The Environment Agency 1996

The Environment Agency took over from the National Rivers Authority in 1996 and now only Richmond Lock still remains under the jurisdiction of the Port of London Authority.

Historical Sources

The Domesday Book (1086)

The Domesday Book was a manuscript record of the Great Survey of England and parts of Wales, completed in 1086 by order of William the Conqueror. According to the Anglo-Saxon Chronicle, his men were sent *'all over England into every single shire to find out how many hides there were in the shire, what land and cattle the king had himself in the shire, what dues he ought to have in twelve months from the shire. He also had a record of how much land his archbishops had, his bishops and his abbots and his earls...'*. It tried to value the nation – the amount of arable land, the number of plough teams (consisting of eight oxen), river meadows, pasture, fishing weirs, water-mills, salt pans etc. Most shires were visited by groups of royal officers who held a public enquiry. Every township was represented as were local lords. The unit of enquiry was the Hundred, a subdivision of the county. The return of each Hundred was sworn by 12 local jurors – six English and six Normans. The survey and audit was written in Latin and clearly established who held what in the wake of the Norman Conquest, clarified what rights and dues were owed to the King and settled the liability of his great barons to provide military resources, in soldiers or in cash, when campaigning.

John Leland (1503 – 1552)

John Leland was an English poet and historian. He used the county as his basic unit for studying the local history of England. He made numerous journeys through England between 1539 and 1543. He collected information from books, chronicles and oral sources on villages, towns and rivers and recorded this in notebooks, known as his 'itinerary'. The latest edition ran to five printed volumes.

John Olgilby (1600 – 1676)

John Olgiby published the first British Road Atlas in 1675. He used the scale of 1 inch to 1 mile. Miles were further divided into furlongs. It was called the *Britannia Atlas*. In it are shown 100 strip maps accompanied by a double-side of text, giving advice on how the map might be used.

Francis Frith (1822 – 1898)

Francis Frith took photographs in the Middle East and, from 1860, embarked on a huge project to photograph every town and village in the UK. He started off by taking the photographs himself and later he hired others to take them for him. He set up a postcard company and ran one of the largest photographic studios in the world.

Henry Taunt (1842–1922)

Henry Taunt photographed Victorian and Edwardian life. Born in St Ebbes, Oxford, he set up his own photographic business in several premises in the city. By 1922 he had a collection of 60,000 glass plate negatives. He published his own survey of '*his beloved river*' in 1872 in his book, *A New Map of the River Thames*. He produced over fifty local histories and guidebooks as well as being a major publisher of postcards. A blue plaque exists on the wall of 393 Cowley Road where he lived from 1889 until his death. He is buried in Rose Hill Cemetery.

Jerome K Jerome (1859—1927)

Three Men in a Boat, the book, written by Jerome K Jerome, was published in 1889 and describes a boating holiday on the Thames between Kingston and Oxford. Its original purpose was as a guidebook and Jerome recounts historical associations with Hampton Court Palace, Magna Carta Island, Monkey Island and recalls humorous anecdotes involving river pastimes like fishing and boating. His ashes are buried in Ewelme churchyard.

Crossing	Page
A419 Road Bridge, Cricklade	15
A429 Road Bridge, Kemble	11
Abingdon Crossings	38
Albert Bridge	83
Appleford Railway Bridge	42
Barnes Railway & Pedestrian Bridge	78
Battersea Bridges	81
Benson Lock & Weir	45
Blackfriars Bridge	89
Blackwall Tunnels	96
Bloomers Hole Footbridge	19
Bourne End Rail Bridge & Walkway	59
Bridges in Ashton Keynes	13
Bridges of Somerfield Keynes	12
Buscot Lock & Weir	20
Canary Wharf to Rotherhithe Ferry	95
Cannon Street Railway Bridge	91
Castle Eaton Bridge	16
Caversham Bridge	51
Chelsea Bridge	84
Chertsey Bridges	68
Chiswick Bridge	78
Clifton Hampden Bridge	42
Cookham Bridge	60
Cricklade Town Bridge	15
Dartford Crossing	99
Donnington Bridge	35
Eaton Hastings Footbridge	20
Emirates Air Line	97
Ewan Bridges	11
Eynsham Lock & Weir	27
Eysey Footbridge	15
Folly Bridge	33
Fulham Railway & Pedestrian Bridge	80
Gasworks Bridge, Oxford	32
Gatehampton Railway Bridge	49
Godstow Bridges	28
Golden Jubilee Bridge	88
Goring & Streatley Bridge	49

Crossing	Page
Grandpont Bridge, Oxford	32
Gravesend to Tilbury Ferry	99
Greenwich Foot Tunnel	96
Grosvenor Railway Bridge	84
Hailstone House Footbridge	13
Halfpenny Bridge, Letchlade	17
Hambledon Lock & Weir	56
Hammersmith Bridge	79
Hammerton's Ferry	73
Hampton Court Bridge	70
Hampton Ferry	70
Hannington Bridge	16
Hart's Weir Footbridge	25
Henley Bridge	55
Hungerford Bridge	88
Iffley Lock & Weir	35
Inglesham Roundhouse Footbridge	17
Isis Road Bridge	36
Kennington Railway Bridge	36
Kew Bridges	77
Kingston Bridges	71
Lambeth Bridge	86
Little Wittenham Crossings	43
London Bridge	92
M4 Thames Bridge	63
M25 & A30 Bridge, Runnymede	67
Maidenhead Bridges	61
Marlow Bridges	58
Medley Footbridge, Oxford	30
Midland & SW Junction Bridge	14
Millennium Footbridge	90
Moulsford Railway Bridge	48
Neigh Bridges	12
New Bridge	25
North Meadow Bridges, Cricklade	14
Nuneham Railway Bridge	38
Old Man's Footbridge	22
Osney Bridges, Oxford	31
Pinkhill Lock & Weir	26

Crossing	Page
Putney Bridge	80
Radcot Bridge	21
Reading Crossings	51
Richmond Bridges	74
Rotherhithe Tunnel	95
Rushey Lock & Weir	22
St John's Bridge	18
Sandford Lock & Footbridge	37
Shepperton to Weybridge Ferry	69
Shifford Cut Bridge & Duxford Ford	24
Shillingford Bridge	44
Shiplake Railway Bridge	54
Sonning Bridge & Backwater Bridges	53
Southwark Bridge	91
Staines Bridge	67
Staines Railway Bridge	68
Summerleaze Footbridge	63
Sutton Courtney Crossings	40
Swinford Toll Bridge	27
Tadpole Bridge	23
Teddington Lock Footbridges	73
Temple Footbridge	57
Tenfoot Footbridge	24
Thames Bridge	28
Tower Bridge	94
Twickenham Bridge	75
Vauxhall Bridge	85
Victoria & Albert Bridges, Datchet	66
Wallingford Bridge	46
Walton Bridge	69
Wandsworth Bridge	81
Water Eaton House Footbridge	16
Waterhay Bridge	13
Waterloo Bridge	88
Westminster Bridge	87
Whitchurch Toll Bridge	50
Windsor Bridges	64
Winterbrook Bridge	47
Woolwich Ferry & Foot Tunnel	98